IMPROVISING VIOLIN

BY JULIE LYONN LIEBERMAN

IMPROVISING VIOLIN

By Julie Lyonn Lieberman

Published by:
Huiksi Music
P.O. box 495
New York, NY 10024

Preface by: Darol Anger
Cover Design and Design Consultation: Loren Moss
Cover Artwork, Loren Ellis   NY, NY
Editor: Nan Gatewood
Graphic Design: Julie Lyonn Lieberman
Photo of Joe Venuti: Milt Hinton
Photo of Dave Balakrishnan: Marvin Collins
Photo of Shankar: Randy Matusow
Group photo of Shankar, Blake, Richards, Williams: Ira Landgarten
Cover Photo of Julie Lyonn Lieberman: Randall Wallace

Copyright 1995 by Huiksi Music
Third Printing
Printed in the United States of America

By Julie Lyonn Lieberman
Includes index.
1. Music   2. Musicians   3. Music Study   4. Violin   5. Improvisation   6. Jazz
7. Jazz Violin   8. Musical Styles   9. Violin Improvisation

ISBN 1-879730-10-3 $19.95 Soft cover
4 5 6 7 8 9 10 Printing 2004

This book is dedicated to the thousands of students I've had the privilege of interacting with over the last twenty years. The work process we've shared has been a richly mutual process of creativity and discovery.

Many thanks to:

Darol Anger, for writing such a thoughtful preface

Dave Balakrishnan for his suggestions and the use of an excerpt of Spider Dreams

Loren Moss, for her splendid cover design and bountiful advice on the look of the book, and, as with the last two projects, her solid moral support and friendship

My editor, Nan Gatewood, for her linguistic wizardry

Loren Ellis, for the beautiful cover art

Milt Hinton, for his photograph of Joe Venuti

Billy Taylor, Milt Hinton, Darol Anger, Dave Balakrishnan, Matt Glaser, Claude Williams, Joe Kennedy, Jr., John Blake, Jr., Howard Armstrong, L. Shankar, and James Emery, for the use of their quotes

Larry and Pam Fishman, Randy of Zeta Music Systems, Stephan Kurmann, and Mark Wood, for their support in the Amplification Chapter

Barrie Edwards and Peter Pickow of Music Sales Corporation

My teachers of improvisation: Sal Mosca, Bobby McFerrin, Ken Guilmartin, Gwen Watson, and my inner muse

PREFACE

When I first met Julie Lieberman almost fifteen years ago, she had already published two books, was working on her first recording, and had a fountain in her room. Not many people even get around to the fountain. Since then, I've seen her produce concerts, give seminars, start and run a non-profit organization, write a musical play, make more recordings, create a major radio series, and make beautiful books designed to encourage, inspire, and connect string players to a great heritage some of us never knew existed.

This book embodies many of her gifts: wide scholarship, the desire to organize, a sense of community, and a deep love of free expression and creativity in music and on the violin. Julie's also an unstoppable "evolver" and "improver" (in the words of cellist Mark Summer), and as she has gained in knowledge and skill, so has this excellent book. I thought it was good when it first came out; I think it's great now.

Julie's a rare combination of dreamer and doer, a free spirit and determined worker. Many improvising string players, regardless of generation or style, can say, "She's done a lot for me." So, friends, let's all thank Julie and get to work!

Darol Anger
Turtle Island String Quartet

TABLE OF CONTENTS

INTRODUCTION

The violin has definitely been a teacher in my life. It's acquainted me with the great composers of our world, led me to folk festivals as a fiddler, insisted on guiding me through the chordal complexities of jazz standards, and introduced me to music as a healing force. Most importantly, the violin has taken me into a realm of creativity, spontaneity and expressivity that I never dreamed existed when I trained as a young classical player.

In the sixties, there were few non-classical role models except in folk music, and there certainly weren't any improvisation-oriented violin books to turn to. Occasionally, a whisper of Stephane Grappelli's name floated across the ocean from Europe. The recordings of Eddie South and Stuff Smith lay buried in the archives (later to be re-released due to popular demand), and few of the dozens of black blues fiddlers from the twenties had made it from 78 vinyl to 45 rpm.

Since the field of jazz violin pedagogy did not yet exist, those of us who hankered for fresh avenues of expression on the instrument had to forge new techniques, new ways of listening, and new mind-sets to guide our hands. By the end of the decade and on into the early seventies, a handful of players such as Sugarcane Harris, Jean Luc Ponty, Michal Urbaniak, L. Shankar, Richard Greene, Jerry Goodman, and Stephane

Grappelli had gained recognition, inspiring a generation of string players.

After fourteen years of classical study, my introduction to improvisation came as a fiddler on the folk music scene in the early seventies, when I began to play backup for various singers. This taste of improvisation inspired me to eight years of study with pianist Sal Mosca, protégé of Lennie Tristano. During this time, I stumbled across the blues fiddle style of Lonnie Johnson. When I discovered that he'd recorded in the late 1920s, I began to investigate the existence of other blues fiddlers. I was surpised to discover that Johnson was one of many recorded blues fiddlers, representing a tradition that reached back into the eighteen hundreds.

Blues Fiddle, my first book, was published in 1979, first by Mel Bay Publications, and then later by Oak Publications. The five years of original research that went into writing that book provided me with a sense of my historical roots as an improviser, as well as a musical and technical context for the evolution of my own style and technique. The response to the book from violinists worldwide convinced me that string players needed more information on improvisation. This realization led me to write the first edition of *Improvising Violin,* which was published in 1984, and to create my National Public Radio series, *The Talking Violin,* which premiered in 1989.

While mass public recognition of the violin in jazz has been slow, the emerging numbers of improvising violinists making records, tapes, TV appearances, method books, instructional tape and video series, or being featured in articles in magazines like *Downbeat* show us that this is all changing. Just as the physical shape of the violin has gradually transformed in response to the demands of the music, we are moving into a time that recognizes the violin as a vital force in original American music. We owe a great debt to the blues fiddlers. These players carried the instrument out of European classical and fiddle literature, and developed it into an improvisational voice in music. Responsible for breathing new life into the instrument, they created a rich tradition of original violin literature.

Above all other aspects of the violin, the one thing that never ceases to amaze me, is how incredibly flexible this instrument is: it's sung the powerful, soulful music of many cultures throughout the world. You can put the same violin into the hands of ten violinists and they're going to make that instrument sound completely different! Today, there are so many improvising string players, that it's dizzying. I'm constantly astounded by the new names and the rising level of capability. Yet, resource materials do not equal those available to guitarists, pianists, or sax players. After being out of print for almost five years, this new, revised edition of *Improvising Violin*, hopes to provide violinists with a comprehensive resource with which they can develop their improvisational abilities.

Whether or not you intend to pursue a professional life as an improvising violinist, I hope that the information in this book provides you with a key to new musical experiences. I welcome you to an exciting journey, and look forward to making a contribution to your path in music.

IMPROVISING VIOLIN: A BRIEF HISTORY

Poughkeepsie Journal, November 24, 1791

RUN AWAY — a Negro man named Robert. 23 years old, about five feet, ten inches high. Speaks good English, is a fiddler and took his fiddle with him.

In the early days of America, the violin may have claimed its popularity based on the accessibility of its parts and how easy and light it was to carry. Some scratchy 78 recordings and old newspaper ads are all that's left of the legacy of slave musicians who learned that excellence on an instrument like the fiddle might provide them with a slightly gentler life than that of a field hand.

Solomon Northup...
a black violinist kidnapped in the North and sold into slavery

Alas! had it not been for my beloved violin, I scarcely can conceive how I could have endured the long years of bondage. It introduced me to great houses—relieved me of many days labor in the field—supplied me with conveniences for my cabin—with pipes and tobacco, and extra pairs of shoes, and oftentimes led me away from the presence of a hard master, to witness scenes of jollity and mirth. Often, at midnight, when sleep had fled affrighted from the cabin, and my soul was disturbed and troubled by the contemplation of my fate, it would sing me a song of peace.

While slaves entertained their masters by playing square dance tunes and classical music, their own music evolved into the twelve-bar form we now call the blues. The violin actually played an important role in the evolution of the blues. By the early thirties, there were over fifty recorded blues fiddlers, so we can assume that there were actually hundreds in existence throughout the South. Almost all of the blues fiddlers that recorded did so between 1924 and 1931 (with a few exceptions like Lonnie Chatmon of the Mississippi Sheiks and Curtis Mosby, both of whom recorded as late as 1934). Some old-timers, like Henry Son Sims, Carl Martin, Howard Armstrong and Butch Cage, lived long enough to fiddle the country blues in later decades.

Due to racism, blacks couldn't record on the same label as whites. Okeh Records (later to become Columbia) was the first record company to create a separate label for blacks, called "Race Records." Along with Clifford Hayes, Lonnie Johnson and his brother James "Steady Roll" were among the first of the violinists that Okeh recorded. Because 78 records only allowed for a little over three minutes per side, most groups developed a standard arrangement to fit into that time. Groups using fiddle tended to open with a fiddle intro, go on to a sung verse or two, a fiddle solo, a few more sung verses, and then a tag usually played by the fiddler.

There are few people left to remember the unrecorded fiddle styles of Frank Martin (who was sold twice as a slave), Steve Todder of Tennessee, Jack Scaggs, or Henry Alexander. Some players, like Milton Robie, Charlie Pierce and Tom "Bluecoat" Nelson, recorded very few sides. John Gadd, a mulatto who taught at the University of Cincinatti, band leader and violinist Jimmy Bell, Clarence Moore of Chicago, and jazz violinists Burns Campbell, Reg Smith, and Al Duffy are just some of the many undocumented blues and early jazz violinists.

There were also the more popular players, like Eddie Anthony, who played in Peg Leg Howell's band; Will Batts, who recorded with Jack Kelly; George Bell and Leroy Parker, who both played with Mamie Smith; and Curtis Mosby, who fiddled in Roosevelt Syke's band. These players made it onto vinyl, but were lost when 45 LP's bypassed the 78s.

In all instances, we can make some generalizations about the techniques these violinists evolved to move the instrument into a new stylistic framework. Classical techniques like vibrato and tremolo were adapted to play the blues: the width and speed of the vibrato became more varied, and tremolo became a blues shimmer. Various slide techniques were developed, and, of course, each player had to learn how to improvise. Some adaptations are more difficult to verbalize due to their extreme subtlety. For instance, rather than attacking notes in a symmetrical, crisp fashion, the use of the bowing arm, coupled with a left-hand slide technique, created an effect that was more like a snake ambling and slithering its way along.

Rhythmic emphasis shifted from symmetrical rhythms to swung and syncopated ones.

Alan Jabbour...
Director of the National Folklife Center

In the early sixties I was at Duke University as a graduate student, and I set out on a mission to find and record old time fiddle players of the upper South. The fiddle players I recorded were all white fiddle players, mostly old men. Most of them are dead now, I'm afraid. But as I recorded and learned to play from them, I also studied up on the history of the tunes that they were playing, and the history of the whole style of the region of the upper South. The more I studied the style, the more I realized that it wasn't simply an Anglo-American style.

For one thing, most dramatically, I noticed that the bowing patterns of all the fiddlers I visited were filled with complicated, elaborate syncopations. Those syncopations were not something that they added onto their music just to make it lively. It was their music. That was the way they thought music. It was imbedded very deeply in their style. And these were men who had learned to play the fiddle in the late 19th century...before jazz, before blues, even before ragtime. Where I think they learned it was from the black fiddlers who participated deeply in the tradition of fiddling in the early 19th century. We know that though there are few black fiddlers today, in the late 18th and early 19th century, there were as many black as white fiddlers throughout the South. And blacks participated in the very creation of the style of fiddling we now think of as Southern fiddling. And it's clear that no other part of the English speaking world has these complicated syncopated patterns. It's clearly an Afro-American contribution to fiddling.

Keep in mind that recording a few sides now and then and playing at picnics and square dances wasn't enough to survive. Some violinists farmed full-time while others migrated up to cities like Chicago to get better work. At first, city violinists found excellent jobs playing for the silent films. They were able to buy their own homes and dress well.

---
66   99

Milt Hinton...jazz bassist

Chicago had all these great violin players, black violin players. Every theater had an orchestra play the music for the screen, because there was no sound. So in every orchestra there would usually be a violin, a drum, and a piano. In 1929, Al Jolson made "The Jazz Singer", which was the first movie with sound attached to it. And with the coming of that, every theater got rid of all the musicians.

But the violin players had no place to go. There were loads of black clubs in Chicago for black musicians to work in, but they didn't use violins. These were night clubs, so there was no room for violins. So this was the end...1930, 31, 32, 33...was the end of the black violin players. All of these wonderful violin players—they disappeared.

In those days, I delivered papers. I'd go around to peoples' homes and collect for my paper, the Chicago Herald Examiner. And I'd usually go to the back door. There I found them. Since they didn't have any more work playing violin, they were making cigars on their screened-in back porches; they were rolling cigars and taking them downtown to sell them to the wealthy people in the downtown department stores. This is how they survived.

Once blues fiddlers could no longer work playing for the silent films, blues and jazz violin went underground for over a decade. This was primarily because black string players weren't allowed into the all white orchestras, the violin couldn't compete with the volume of the horn players and rhythm sections in the blues and jazz clubs, and the technology wasn't yet available for violin amplification. In fact, outside of the early work of Joe Venuti, Stuff Smith, and Eddie South, the only evidence we have in the late thirties of improvised violin is in police arrest reports: some violinists were earning their living playing in the red light district!

With the invention of pickups and the advent of the use of mikes and amps in clubs, violins began to re-emerge onto the scene. They appeared in Big Band settings in the capable hands of players like Ray Nance, Jimmy Bell, Ray Perry, and others. Second generation American improvisers such as Butch Cage, Howard Armstrong, Eddie South, Stuff Smith, Joe Venuti, Claude Williams, Michael White, Sugarcane Harris and Papa John Creach had greater technique and knowledge of theory than the earlier players, and took the violin more deeply into improvisation by using it in jazz, swing, and rock music.

Before we explore the rich contributions made by second generation improvising violinists, let's backtrack a moment and look at the black string band tradition, which began before the American Revolution and continued until the 1930s. String band music is worth mentioning here because a good deal of the material involved improvisation on the fiddler's part. Early American string bands performed at picnics, square dances, Saturday night frolics, and family and social gatherings throughout the South. The original bands consisted of fiddle, banjo, guitar and later, mandolin. Most of the early groups had an eclectic repertoire; they played country dance tunes, and later blues, ragtime numbers, popular songs and jazz. Few of these musicians had formal training of any kind. Never lacking in spirit, they came from an aural tradition. Some players, like fiddler Chasey Collins, played with such gusto that you could forgive them their rusty sound.

Some of the groups that were popular in the early thirties, like "The Tennessee Chocolate Drops," could play in any key and had a vast repertoire of original as well as popular folk and blues tunes. This group was made up of mandolinist Carl Martin, guitarist Ted Bogan and fiddler Howard Armstrong. The Tennessee Chocolate Drops disappeared from the music scene for many years, re-emerging as Martin, Bogan and Armstrong in the sixties, when they gained national popularity on the folk music scene. Carl Martin also performed with his own group, "Carl Martin and the Chicago String Band."

He was a good fiddler in his own right as he demonstrated on a tune called "Weeping and Moaning," recorded in 1966.

66 99

Howard Armstrong...blues fiddler

But one day, I told my daddy, "I got to have a violin." He said, "Well, you know, I got nine kids. There's eleven of us in the family. My pay isn't enough to buy you a fiddle. But I tell you what I'll do, son: You go around the trash piles, in the alleys, and see if you can find an old seasoned-out dirt box. And I did. And the old man came in the evening from work (he worked till five o'clock at the blast furnace) and he took a pocket knife, cut me out a violin, and I wish to this day that I had it! He carved the neck out first. And he cut out everything for it but the strings. He cut the bridge out of a piece of hardwood, and round the fringe of the woods where we lived they had dogwood—you know—hard wood trees with those pretty blossoms on it. That tree is hard as ivory, almost! I got him a chunk of that dogwood and he made me a tailpiece, and cut the pegs out, and a thing to bow it; and he varnished it with some—back then they had a kind of varnish you had in can—looked like it was a cross between lacquer and varnish—it dried real fast. They call it "japalac." And it had the color right into the liquid. And he "japalacked" that fiddle for me. I was thrilled to no end! And I almost never, never, never got home, stopping beside the road, playing for the chipmunks, squirrels, and birds...I scared everything, I guess!

Popular groups like the Mississippi Sheiks placed the fiddle in a central position, and for good reason; fiddler Lonnie Chatmon had a solid command of the instrument. In fact, under the guiding influence of Lonnie Chatmon, The Mississippi Sheiks were one of the few professional string bands in the Mississippi area. They performed for white audiences more than black, and according to Sam Chatmon, Lonnie pursued music as a livelihood because he didn't like farming and "...was tired of smelling mule farts"! The Mississippi Sheiks recorded roughly 75 sides in the late twenties and early thirties as well as dozens of others using pseudonyms like The Mississippi Mud Steppers and The Mississippi Hot Footers to get around their record contract.

Today's string bands combine classical and jazz training with composition to create a more sophisticated multilayered sound. The traditional combination of fiddle, guitar and mandolin has developed into all kinds of unusual combinations of string instruments. For instance, the group Black Swan is composed of Akbar Ali on violin, Eileen Folson and Abdul Wadud on cellos, and Reggie Workman on bass. Unlike Black Swan, The String Trio of New York is made up of violin (originally Charles Burnham, now Regina Carter), guitar (James Emery) and bass (John Lindberg). They combine arrangements of popular jazz tunes, premieres of work by contemporary composers, and original works by members of the trio.

Turtle Island String Quartet generates some of the most vibrantly exciting contemporary string band music of our time. Founded by violinists Dave Balakrishnan and Darol Anger, this group also includes viola, with Mark Summer on cello. While they look like a normal chamber group, there is nothing normal about their wide range of stylistic eclecticism. They combine classical, folk, blues, jazz, Indian, traditional and original material with hard driving swing rhythms, and soaring solos to create a highly unique string sound.

―――――― 66 99 ――――――

James Emery...String Trio of New York

When most people think of a string trio they're thinking of the European tradition of violin, viola and cello. Well, we're an American traditional string trio: violin, guitar and bass. And when we formed in 1977 we didn't know that there was a historical precedent for our ensemble. We found out that Pops Foster in New Orleans had led a string trio consisting of violin, guitar and bass, and it was the group that worked more than any other in New Orleans at the birth of our music. So when we came together, it was really for the music first and foremost. We heard the sound and decided to go with it; it was something that we really loved.

―――――― 66 99 ――――――

Dave Balakrishnan...co-founder of Turtle Island String Quartet

One of the elements that we've had to deal with in our string quartet is the problem of assuming the various roles of a standard jazz band. We're playing a lot of jazz-influenced music where you would normally hear piano, bass, drums and a soloist. So here's this little string quartet, four melody instruments, playing this music that is normally a lot larger. We've had to come up with ways of creating that same effect. Mark Summer, the cellist, assumes the role of the bass player. We use a pickup on his cello, so that we can get a wider, lower sound out of the cello—so that it sounds more like a bass. He does a lot of pizzicato.

DAROL ANGER, DAVE BALAKRISHNAN, AND STEPHANE GRAPPELLI

Darol Anger is the rhythm violin virtuoso, and he's come up with ways of throwing the bow on the strings close to the bridge; it sounds like a snare drum, or a high-hat cymbal. And he's taught the rest of us how to do this. I do a lot of voicing, the harmonic underpinning on which the soloist needs to solo, and, of course, all of us solo. So, we really do work on portraying the sound of a jazz band inside the context of the string quartet, and I think it works.

In the innovative string band groups of today such as The Uptown String Quartet, The Soldier String Quartet, and Kronos, we see a wonderful balance between composition and improvisation. It's truly astonishing to hear such versatility and originality taking place. There are no formulas any more. With a decline in interest in classical string music, and in funding for school string programs, perhaps we can look forward to a revitilization of interest in string music as string players leave the traditional mold, explore their creativity, and develop new technical and stylistic innovations.

The string band tradition seemed to attract violinists who were unschooled in the traditional sense. The music was less demanding harmonically. But as jazz influences grew, the blues fiddle tradition combined with a more finely developed technical capability, and a handful of jazz violinists emerged. Eddie South, Stuff Smith, Joe Venuti, and Stephane Grappelli were the best known of this group.

Eddie South (Edward Otha South) was born in 1904, in Louisiana, Missouri. He attended school in Chicago and started studying the violin with Charlie Elgar when he was ten years old. He went on to study at the Chicago College of Music with Petrowitsch Bissing when he was sixteen. His early professional engagements included performances with Charlie Elgar's band, work as the musical director of Jimmie Wade's Syncopators, and a short stint with Erskine Tate and His Orchestra. It was a tour with Marian Harris that took him to Europe. Even though the tour fell apart, it served an important purpose: his introduction to Europe opened educational and professional doors that were not available to a man of color in America.

South stayed in Europe long enough to study with Firman Touche at the Paris Conservatory as well as with gypsy violinist Jazoz Derzo at the Budapest Conservatory. He also recorded in Paris with guitarist Django Reinhardt and jazz violinist Stephane Grappelli in 1937 shortly before returning to the U.S. Although he did have

66 99

Billy Taylor, jazz pianist and educator

Eddie South was a remarkable musician. He had the discipline that he acquired from his classical training but he had all of that freedom that goes with jazz improvisation. He combined those elements in ways that every musician—on any instrument—could combine them. He had something that was unique to the violin, yet he added a great deal to the jazz vocabulary. He was the first musician I worked with who frequently moved people to tears. He played those gypsy melodies so authentically that the King of the Gypsies used to come and hear us. He'd come in with his whole entourage and they'd sit there and cry.

66 99

Milt Hinton, jazz bassist

Eddie South's technique was absolutely impeccable. He was no accident. He didn't just pick up a violin like I think perhaps Stuff Smith did, or some of the guys before Eddie that didn't have the academic training that Eddie South had. And so he consequently used his academic training to improve on his improvisation...so that his improvisation was played all over the violin. And keys, of course, meant nothing to him. His soul, as far as artistry...his heart was so warm. He was just such a warm player. There ain't no question that they called him a black gypsy. I'm a very old man, and I've never forgotten these things. I can sing his tunes and then know I'm in the same keys he played them in. And this was back in the 30s. He was just that impressive.

some radio gigs in the forties and a television show in the fifties, Eddie South's dark skin forced him to settle for night clubs and second rate theatres even though he was fully cap.ble of a sparkling concert career.

---
66 99

Matt Glaser, jazz violinist and educator

Eddie South was a phenomenally fine classical violinist, who, for reasons both of interest and of prejudice, ended up playing jazz. At the time that he was a master classical violinist, there were real color barriers against a black man playing the Tchaikovsky Violin Concerto in Carnegie Hall. But he also loved jazz and had an extremely unique style of playing it. He played with a phenomenal technique, and a very intense bow attack. He used a lot of glottal sound in his attack, but in slower pieces he tended towards gypsy-like rhapsodizing. In faster pieces he had a very unique sense of swing, and a very unique improvisational style in which he would take motifs and displace them by octaves.

There are a couple of recordings of Eddie South with Django Reinhardt that were made in Paris in the 1930s, as well as a famous duet with Stephane Grappelli in which they played the Bach Double Violin Concerto. And this was a notorious piece of music, because it was banned by the Nazis as being a prime example of cultural decadence. They publically displayed a meltdown of the master tape! So for a long time it was very difficult to hear the recording. All the issues that are available on the market now, are from people's home laquers that they remastered onto a record.

When South performed, he'd often lead with a blues or jazz tune, switch to a classical piece of music and then end with a gypsy air. His fluidly swung lines, full-bodied tone, evenly paced vibrato, and command of the instrument in a number of styles distinguish his sound. Unfortuntately, even though he recorded a handful of albums, his only solo album in America was "The Dark Angel of the Violin." South died on April 25, 1962.

According to Billy Taylor, Eddie South and Stuff Smith were good friends. In 1944 Taylor had been accompanying South for about a month and had never met Stuff. They were performing at a club called Elmers in Chicago and were playing their regular show. All of a sudden, Eddie began to play the blues and all of his jazz repertoire! This wasn't what they normally played. Taylor couldn't imagine what caused the sudden change. "When the set was over, he introduced me to Stuff Smith. I said, 'Oh! That's what that was all about!' Later that evening, we went over to hear Stuff and his trio. And this was the trio with John Levy on bass and Jimmy Jones on piano that I'm speaking of. Stuff began to play 'Claire de Lune' and I thought, 'You guys have gotta be kidding.' That was not his bag. Nor was it Eddie's bag to do what Stuff did. But that was their way of paying homage to each other."

Stuff Smith (Hezekiah Leroy Gordon Smith), who was born in August, 1909, in Portsmouth, Ohio, played in a style that was more gut bucket, as it's often called, or bluesy. Inspired by Louis Armstrong, he left classical music for a career as a jazz violinist. When Stuff was forced to leave Jelly Roll Morton's group because he couldn't be heard above the horns, he began experimenting with amplification. As far as we know, he was actually the first improvising violinist to go electric!

Milt Hinton

It's the rhythm that's most important. So that's the kind of thing I would say about Stuff Smith. He was growling…his bow would bite into the strings. And he was very durable. He played a long time, strictly jazz. He'd take 25, 30 choruses. And he just went on and on. It wasn't academic in the sense of that, but it was just absolutely fantastic. And in a club where everyone was listening to saxophones, and drums, and trumpets, he had to do this in order to be heard. He was unique in that he was the only one who was doing this kind of thing, because Eddie South didn't play in these kind of places. His places were more sedate and sadiddy, where people sat and listened. People were drinking beer and having a ball where Stuff Smith was playing. And he loved the ladies: he'd be juggling a lady and playing with one finger at the same time. He was known for that. He was quite a ladies' man.

Billy Taylor

When I worked with Stuff Smith in the Onyx Club and we played concerts in Town Hall, the one thing that impressed me was the manner in which he reached the audience. He really made them pat their feet, clap their hands, and respond. He was really a musician who communicated in the best sense of the word.

Up against the same racist climate that Eddie South had to struggle with, Stuff Smith spent the late thirties performing at the Onyx Club on 52nd Street in Manhattan. In the forties, he bounced between Chicago and New York. By this point in time, his health, due to alcoholism and heavy touring, began to deteriorate. Each tour to Europe seemed to take a greater toll upon his energies, until the last few trips culminated in total collapse and subsequent hospitalization. He died in Munich on September 25th, 1967. Out of all the improvising violinists from the first half of the century, I find Stuff Smith's style on the violin the most distinctive and unique. The rhythmic aspect of what he did was incredibly intense and exciting. He knew how to coax the full range of human emotion out of his instrument; he wasn't afraid to make sounds that were textured or rough. He used a small portion of his upper bow in combination with a lot of slurring, and jumped to his frog for some very hard playing so that you heard a lot of rosin and double stops. Stuff Smith was the quintessential swinger.

Ironically, both Eddie South and Stuff Smith died at the age of 58. Neither of them had the opportunities as black jazz musicians in America that their white counterpart, jazz violinist Joe Venuti, had. In fact, Billy Taylor is convinced that both of them died of broken hearts. The following story, told to me by Milt Hinton, typifies what it was like to be an outstanding musician, yet not be able to garner the recognition and respectful treatment that was clearly merited on both their parts.

In the early thirties, Joe Venuti recommended that Paul Whiteman use Eddie South to replace him. Joe had been accompanying the singer Bea Palmer and she was very attached to hearing his jazz violin accompaniment behind her as she sang. Venuti wanted to go out on his own, and even though he knew in those days there was no mixing of races, he told Whiteman that Eddie South was the only violinist he knew of who could really replace him. Palmer was so insistent about being accompanied by violin that they hired Eddie South and then placed him behind a screen on the stage to accompany her anonymously!

Joe Venuti's career, on the other hand, spanned six decades and included roughly two dozen records. He started performing in the early 20s and it was obvious from his first recording that he had a highly developed jazz violin sound. One of Joe Venuti's earliest collaborations was with jazz guitarist Eddie Lang, which lasted twelve years until Lang's premature death in 1933. After Lang's death, Venuti performed with a number of different guitarists, Big Bands, and various ensembles, before he began touring under his own name.

Always reaching for perfection as a violinist and a jazz musician, Venuti's albums are unique in that he collaborated with many different jazz artists in his constant exploration of the instrument and the art form. Venuti even invented a new bow technique early in his career. He took the pin out of the end of his bow, placed the hair across all four strings and played beautifully thought-out three- and four-note chords.

JOE VENUTI

(He used this technique in his 1975 recording of "C-Jam Blues.")

Venuti was filled with humor and love. There are many stories about the jokes he played on his fellow musician, such as the time that he booked every major bass player in New York City to play the same gig, and had them arrive at the same time on the same street corner as he watched from a hotel window with delight. The union had the last laugh, though, because it made him pay all of them!

I had no idea, when I heard him perform with tremendous energy at Michael's Pub here in New York City to a crowded house (where he was joined by numerous jazz celebrities who had come to hear him play and had been invited up to sit in), that he was dying. He passed away shortly after that engagement from cancer in August 1978. Reports on his birth date range from 1894 to 1904, so his age at death was unknown. Always young in

SHANKAR, JOHN BLAKE JR., VICKI RICHARDS, CLAUDE WILLIAMS
AT THE 1988 THIRD AMERICAN JAZZ STRING SUMMIT

spirit, he is remembered fondly by many musicians and fans.

French jazz violinist Stephane Grappelli paralleled Venuti's development, in that he recorded his first album in the early 20s with legendary guitarist Django Reinhardt and the Hot Club of France. Their work together was classic. To date, Grappelli has recorded well over one hundred albums. Grappelli even recorded with Stuff Smith in Paris, which is a particularly interesting recording to listen to because of how they influenced each other stylistically.

Grappelli has been the most prolific of the jazz violinists worldwide. Probably the easiest through the years for classical violinists to relate to as a stepping stone into improvisation because of his classical sound on the instrument, his warmth as a person is embodied in his sweet, warm tone and classical-style vibrato.

I distinctly remember hearing him perform at Carnegie Hall in the early seventies. He was the first jazz violinist I'd ever heard live, and the continuity of his phrases, combined with the fluidity of his technique, filled me with excitement and inspiration. Although I personally came to prefer a more horn-like quality on violin in jazz, I've always had tremendous respect for Grappelli's tremendous contribution to the field of jazz violin.

EARLY JAZZ VIOLINISTS: LESSER KNOWN PLAYERS

While Eddie South, Stuff Smith, Stephane Grappelli, and Joe Venuti did achieve significant recognition back in the thirties and forties, other players like Jimmy Bell, Al Duffy and Clarence Moore were passed by. Emilio Caceres, who only recorded about four sides, demonstrated tremendous technique and gusto in his 1937 recording of "Jig in G" with his brother Ernie on clarinet. Both Ray Nance, who was known for his work on trumpet and Ray Perry for his alto sax, played excellent jazz violin as well. There's also the phenomenal jazz violin style of Svend Asmussen. He was introduced to American audiences through Duke Ellington's album, "Jazz Violin Session," in which Asmusen, Ray Nance, and Stephane Grappelli were presented as soloists as well as in a group jam. Svend Asmussen's extreme popularity in Europe has prevented him from pursuing a performance reputation here in the U.S., but some of his recordings are available here.

There are only two players on the scene who spanned the evolution of the violin from the black blues lineage, across the early jazz violin players, on into our time: Claude Williams and Joe Kennedy, Jr. Claude Williams began his career on fiddle with Andy Kirk in the twenties and later became famous as a jazz guitarist with the Count Basie band in the forties, only to return to the violin. His violin solo on Jay McShann's recording of "Hootie Blues," made in 1972, exemplifies a lineage that started with the blues fiddlers of the twenties, but includes the best of rhythm and blues, as well as Kansas City jazz.

66 99

Claude Williams, jazz violinist

Like I tell everybody about my brother-in-law, he's the one who started me out in everything. He'd be sitting around the house playing the blues on an old guitar and get tired and lay it down. I'd pick up the guitar and almost play the same thing. When he saw I was interested, he taught me the mandolin and then the cello. A cello isn't usually the right type of instrument for a string band, so they put bass strings on the cello for me to play bass. We'd go around to different barber shops and hotels to play, and somebody would have to carry my cello for me. I was too small to carry it.

Finally, I heard him tell my mother he's gonna get something that never would go out of style. So, he took the cello down and traded it for a violin. And then he brought it home that evening, about 5 or 6 o'clock. Well, I knew how to play the fingering on it. All I had to get was the bowing part. I think the first number I played was "Got to See Your Mama Every Night Or You Can't See Your Mama At All!"

Along with Claude Williams, Joe Kennedy Jr. is one of the last of the great hard-swinging jazz violinists of the swing era. Kennedy is a tremendous player. He's equally at home in swing, blues, jazz and classical. Denied even the right to audition for the local white symphony orchestra when he was ready to enter the professional sphere, he would play in Europe during the summers with his cousin Benny Carter. Now head of the jazz department at Virginia Polytechnic, Joe Kennedy is swinging more than ever.

JOE KENNEDY

Joe Kennedy, Jr., jazz violinist

I have been influenced more by horns and keyboards, although when I was coming along in the early portion of my career I recall the fine work of Stephane Grappelli of the Hot Club of France, and the marvelous work of Eddie South, Joe Venuti and Stuff Smith. In my case, I wanted to play bebop and I just loved listening to Charlie Parker, to Diz Gillespie, Thelonius Monk and people of that time, and I just leaned toward horns, leaned towards pianists -- Art Tatum, Benny Carter -- and this has been my focal point, even now. I love to play with horns and I'm used to playing in six and seven flats (laughs) because those types of keys are a little more comfortable maybe and compatible to horns. The late Bud Johnson used to laugh about that. He'd say 'Joe, you don't play violin, you play tenor saxophone like me!'

By the 1950s, rhythm and blues had gained popularity. With the invention of amplification and violin pickups, violinists could now play with a rhythm section without being drowned out! Remo Biondi, who recorded in the forties and fifties typified this new R&B style, as did artists like Sugarcane Harris, Papa John Creach, and early Clarence

Gatemouth Brown. In addition, a country swing tradition evolved parallel to the swing and jazz violinists. Richard Greene's work in the rock style with Sea-Train was also an important departure from the norm.

Darol Anger

I was never that thrilled with so-called classical music. I was a lot more interested in what was happening on the radio. I was listening to the radio all the time, but I never actually made the connection that I could do that on the violin. I just felt like they were two totally separate worlds until I heard a rock and roll group that happened to have a violin in it. And that was Sea-Train, in about 1970. And I think Richard Green was my opening experience. He was playing the electric violin at the time, and just got me into the idea of doing a whole lot of things on the violin that I only envisioned being able to do on the electric guitar.

Other players, like Bob Wills and Benny Thomasson, and then later, Vassar Clements, influenced generations of folk fiddlers. Many of these violinists, like Vassar Clements, incorporated improvisation with great skill and creativity into the folk fiddle idiom. Mark O'Connor, now in his thirties, began performing and winning fiddle competitions when he was in his early teens. Inspired by the Texas swing fiddle style of Benny Thomasson, O'Connor has evolved his own synthesis of folk, swing and blues. While Joe Kennedy Jr. is a descendant of a black blues and jazz fiddling tradition that reaches back over one hundred years, fiddler Mark O'Connor reflects the use of blues scales and swing music as it was translated into a Texas fiddle style. He represents the next generation of improvising folk fiddlers.

WORLD MUSIC

The sixties brought eastern music to America. Suddenly we heard sitar on Beatles songs, world music concerts and a shift in jazz to include the use of eastern scales. One of the earliest improvising violinists to explore this wedding of world culture was rock violinist Jerry Goodman in his work with The Flock, and then with the Mahavish- nu Orchestra in the early seventies. Since then, improvising violinists such as Jean Luc Ponty, L. Shankar, Steve Kindler, Vicki Richards, and cellist David Darling have experimented with combining technology, world music and improvisation to create new sounds for strings.

Jean Luc Ponty's career has actually spanned bebop jazz, rock, and world music. The best known of this group of players, Ponty was born on September 29, 1942 in Auranches, France. He trained classically with his father, and then at the Paris Conservatory. Inspired by his love for jazz, and his appreciation for the jazz violin styles of Stephane Grappelli as well as Stuff Smith, he moved into jazz full time upon graduation from the Conservatory. He was one of the first owners of the Barcus Berry electric violin, and gradually moved to the cutting edge of technological exploration in his music by using various effects on his electric violin.

In the early part of his career, he, more than any other violinist, created a musical bridge from swing violin to a real bebop violin sound. In essence, his first album, "Sunday Walk," became an icon for how to play modern jazz on violin for a whole generation of improvising violinists. Then Ponty moved on into a more commercial venue and his brief flirtation with jazz violin was traded for amplified, technologically enhanced rock violin in a sophisticated, highly arranged band setting.

The use of eastern scales and bowing techniques, improvisation using one scale rather than harmonic changes, and a meditative or spatial quality was introduced into the American mainstream by Indian violinist L. Shankar. His early recordings with Frank Zappa and John McLaughlin (and the group Shakti) helped establish him in America.

L. Shankar...Indian and rock violinist

The Western violin came as an instrument to India only two hundred years ago when the British arrived. At that time they had the orchestra and so the Indian violinists learned from them, and then retuned the violin and adapted it for Indian music. Since the violin is fretless, you can really bring out all of the Indian ornamentations and the feeling and soul of the music.

The violin is an extension of me; it's part of me. I've been playing for many years...since I was five. My father would first sing a phrase and then I was supposed to imitate it. By doing this, you really start training your ear, so that whatever you hear you're able to remember in your inner ear, much like photographic memory.

My double violin is ten string, stereophonic. It has two necks and two bodies so you can have each neck equalized, and you can have two separate amps and therefore have two different sounds. While playing one neck, the other one serves as sympathetic strings and visa versa; one neck is in the range of the bass and cello while the other one is like viola and violin so that I can get different kinds of sounds.

To turn the tables around, improvising violinist Vicki Richards was one of the first American violinists accepted in India performing Indian music. She has blended her background as a classical and jazz violinist to create her own unique music.

In addition to experimenting with the juxtaposition of electronic effects and world music to create new compositions, some violinists have been bringing these sounds back into the standard classical repertoire. Steve Kindler, best known for his work with internationally acclaimed New Age composer Kitaro, exemplifies this exploration of the violin.

SHANKAR

In the late sixties and early seventies violinist Leroy Jenkins found a way to stretch the instrument in yet another direction. His collaborations with Anthony Braxton, Muhal Richard Abrams and Cecil Taylor, among others, led him into avant garde jazz. As he explored unconventional technical and structural approaches, Jenkins began to compose works for violin and viola shaped around textural motifs. His protege, Billy Bang, has also contributed innovative bow and left-hand techniques through his explorations of avant garde violin music.

Unlike the blues fiddlers from the twenties, today's players perform under their own names and compose most of the music they perform. John Blake Jr., known for his earlier work with McCoy Tyner and Grover Washington, has developed a strong reputation as one of the major jazz violinists of the time.

JOHN BLAKE, JR.

" "

John Blake, Jr., jazz violinist

What music is to me...well, I know that it's a chance to really communicate with people on a higher level that enables you to touch them in perhaps ways that cannot be said in words. Music, for me, is something that touches people in a way that makes them feel better. Almost like healing, in a way, something that inspires them, or something that I'm able to share with them, through my own experiences, that in some way enriches their lives.

Well, the feeling of creating something right at that moment and the feeling that you are doing what you feel at that moment, it's a very emotional feeling for me, because I'm an emotional player, for the most part. Even when I was playing classical music, I was an emotional player. But the closeness that I feel to the instrument, well, it becomes an extension of myself and the way that I'm feeling at that moment.

There are also a group of violinists who have evolved their own unique music, music that's difficult to categorize. For example, violinist Darol Anger is an extremely creative and active talent on the violin.

The past few decades have produced so many talented American and European improvising violinists in so many different styles, that it would be impossible to cover all of them in depth here. For instance, artists like Michal Urbaniak, Didier Lockwood, Terry Jenoure, Nigel Kennedy, Karen Briggs, Matt Glaser, Andy Stein, Noel Pointer, Will Taylor, Jason Hwang, Regina Carter, Rob Thomas, Randy Sabien, Scarlet Rivera, and Mark Wood, to name a few, have each made outstanding contributions to the field. Books and films have emerged on the subject of violin improvisation as well as albums and String Summits, all bringing national attention to the field.

I think that the violin has finally emerged as an equal partner in improvisatory styles to instruments like the guitar, piano, and saxophone. Now we must encourage our conservatories and music schools to finally catch up with the times, and offer string improvisation classes as a part of the regular curriculum!

As you work on developing your unique playing style, try to listen to as many improvising violinists (past and current) as possible. Each of them spent years forging their own creative path on the violin, and it's useful as well as inspiring to familiarize yourself with all of the possible sounds available on the instrument.

CLAUDE WILLIAMS (kneeling), PAUL PEABODY, MATT GLASER, JOHN BLAKE JR., JULIE LYONN LIEBERMAN, BETH COHEN, MARK O'CONNNOR AT THE BERKLEE SPRING STRING FLING

JULIE LYONN LIEBERMAN, VICKI RICHARDS, AND BETTY MACDONALD AT THE THIRD AMERICAN STRING SUMMIT

BUILDING A FOUNDATION

The violin is a versatile and expressive instrument and can do everything a voice or horn can do in improvisation. Since most violinists have been limited to learning how to play from sheet music, their mental and physical training has fostered a "follow the dots" approach rather than one of origination. Sadly, this form of training has weakened listening skills and strengthened visual ones! Learning how to improvise, if you've been trained classically, can easily be approached with that same mind-set: "Teach me the rules. Give me something to follow visually, that will suddenly transform my style of playing." It is essential, however, to approach improvisation with a different mindset and different practice habits.

Improvisation requires the ability to hear a musical line in your inner ear and instantaneously reproduce it on your instrument. Furthermore, improvisation on a tune requires a thorough knowledge of the melody, as well as a working knowledge of the harmonic (chordal) structure of the music. The next section in this book is devoted to providing you with mental and physical techniques to build the technical and creative skills necessary to become a good, or maybe even great, improviser.

PLAYING ON CHORD CHANGES

Most folk, pop, blues, and jazz melodies in and of themselves are often quite simple to play, technically speaking. The greatest challenge in learning how to improvise is to be able to look at a chord chart for a song, know which notes constitute the primary tones of the chord (1 3 5 7), know where they are on the violin, and be able to play the appropriate notes for each chord's complimentary scale (diatonically, meaning scalewise, as well as intervalically, moving in various arpeggiated steps like thirds, fourths, and so on). This requires mastering all twelve keys in all scale and chord forms during your preparatory work! If this sounds like a lot of work, it is...but don't get scared off. It's worth it. Think of this process as a learning curve. It will be slow going at first, but the more you learn, the faster you will learn. Here's how this works:

From the 12-bar blues to the 32-bar jazz tune, after the melody is played, the chord changes become the governing factor in the improvisation. Each chord informs you as to what scale to use for improvisation for the corresponding number of beats; i.e. if the tune opens with a measure of C major followed by a measure of F7 (F dominant seventh), you'll use the notes of a C major scale during the first four beats of your improvisation, and then the notes of an F major scale with a flatted seventh for the next four beats, and so on.

As we've just discussed, when approaching chord changes for a tune, you must first start by learning the primary tones (1 3 5 7) of each chord, since they are the most important building blocks in your improvisation. It's equally important to have the entire scale at your fingertips. Diatonic practice, meaning playing in scalewise or step-like form, requires running the scale two to three octaves up and down as smoothly as possible at all tempos.

It's just as essential to create a mental map of the key as to program the notes into muscle memory. To accomplish this, practice each key mentally away from your instrument, before actually playing it. For instance, if you are playing a tune that requires knowledge of an Ab7 chord, you would start by playing the chord tones (Ab, C, Eb, Gb), then you would visualize playing each note of the scale while naming it, and then you would go back to your instrument to actually play the scale.

First, start with the major scales in all twelve keys. Each chord symbol basically tells you how to alter a major scale. For instance, as long as you are clear about the notes in the A major scale, it's comparatively easy to flat or sharp certain tones within the scale according to the dictates of the chord symbol. Here is a chart that organizes the twelve major keys into a system for memorization. Notice the sharp keys move up in fifths, while the flat keys move down in fifths.

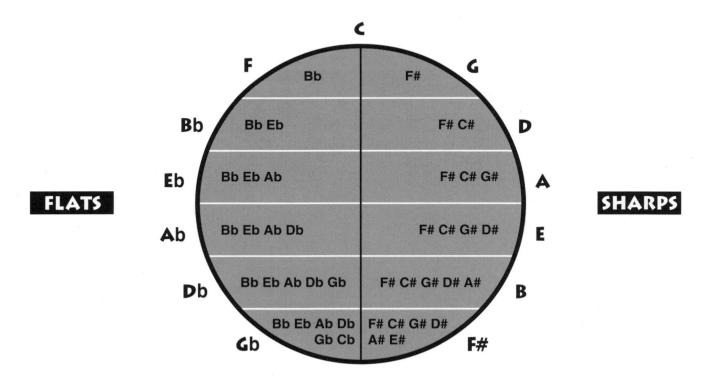

Although there are many types of chords, the seven basic chord types, are: major seventh, major sixth, minor sixth, dominant seventh, minor seventh, diminished seventh, and augmented seventh. When you are improvising, each chord's symbol tells you how to alter the notes of the major scale in that key:

Name	Symbol	Chord	Scale
Major seventh	M7	1 3 5 7	1 2 3 4 5 6 7
Major sixth	M6	1 3 5 6	1 2 3 4 5 6 7
Minor sixth	m6	1 b3 5 6	1 2 b3 4 5 6 7
Dominant seventh	7	1 3 5 b7	1 2 3 4 5 6 b7
Minor seventh	m7	1 b3 5 b7	1 2 b3 4 5 6 b7
Diminished seventh	°7	1 b3 b5 bb7	whole step / half step / w / h / etc.
Augmented seventh	+7	1 3 #5 b7	whole tone scale (all whole steps)

Additional Chords

Names: m7b5...ø...half diminished

Scale: 1 b2 b3 4 b5 b6 b7

Names: dim...diminished...o

Scale: whole step, half step, whole, half, W / H / W / H

Names: 7b9...diminished

Scale: half, whole, H / W / H / W / H / W

Names: minor/major...min maj...m(maj)...-Δ

Scale: 1 2 b3 4 5 6 7

Names: 7+9...altered...alt...diminished whole tone scale...super locrian

Scale: 1 b2 #2 3 #4 #5 b7 (H / W / H / W / W / W / W)

On the following twelve pages, you will find a more complete reference chart for some of the most commonly used chords and their companion scales:

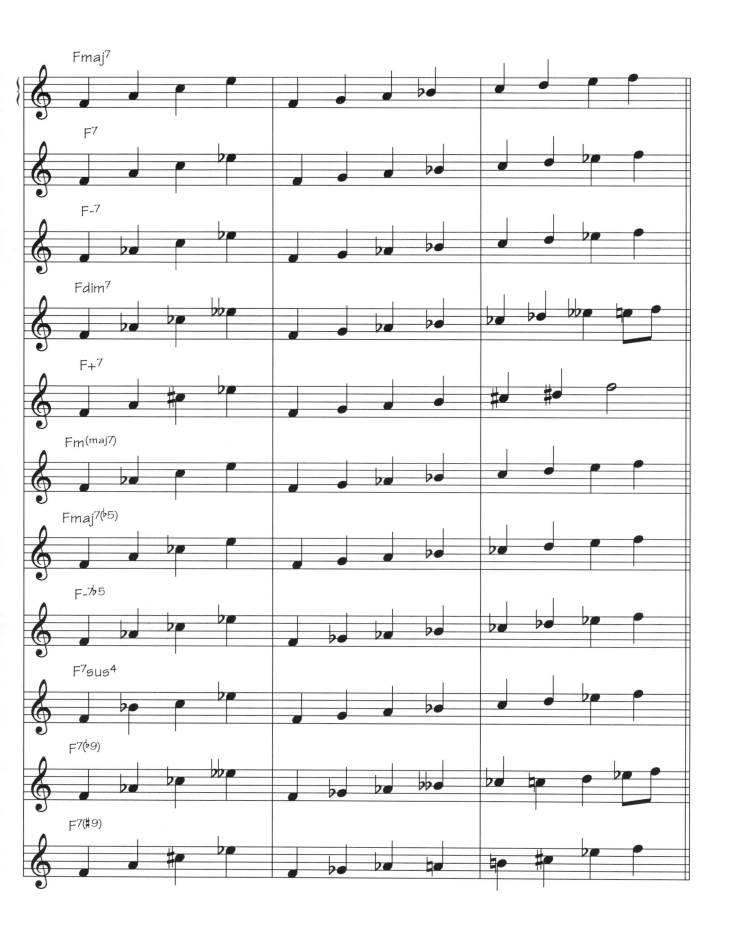

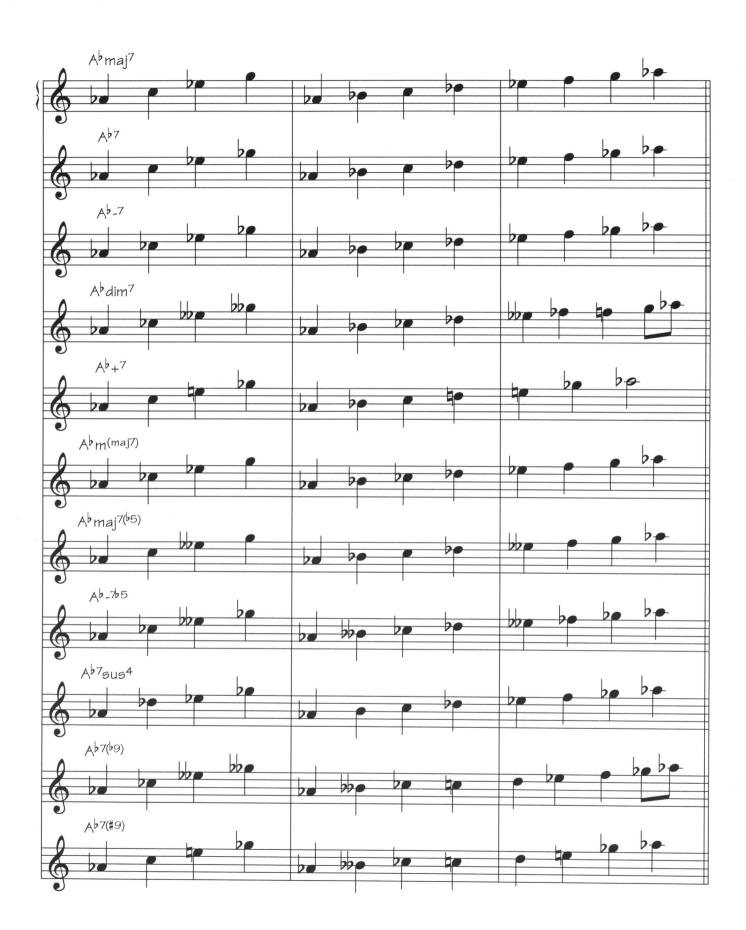

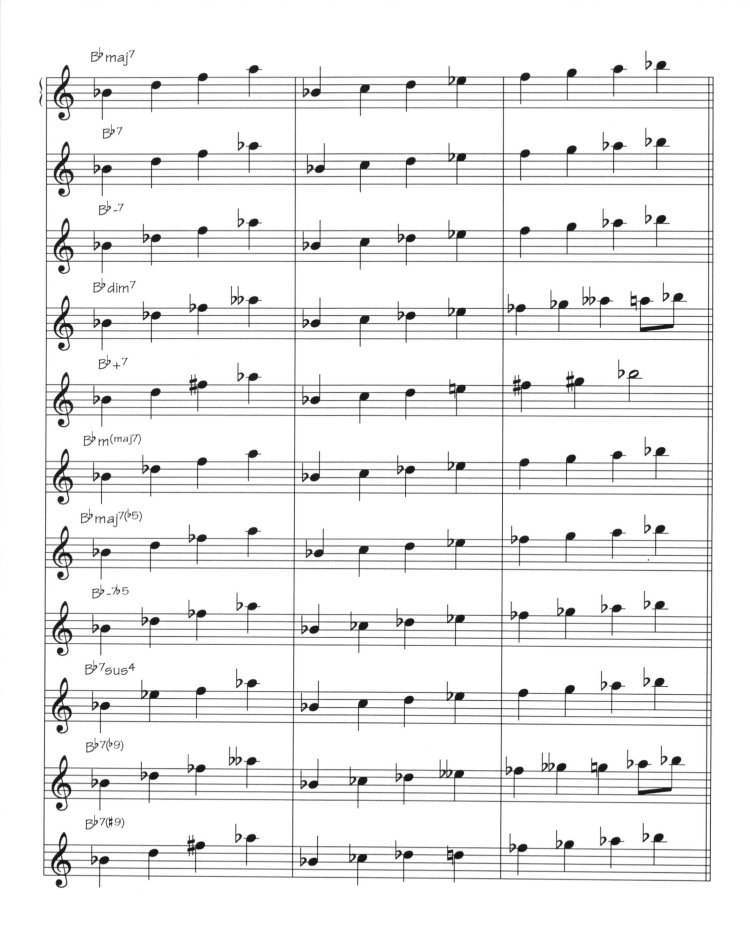

GUIDELINES FOR LEARNING A TUNE

In everything you do to build your improvisatory skills on a given tune, it's best to first memorize the melody and then the chord changes. Reading from paper discourages listening as well as imaging (picturing where the notes are on the fingerboard) and then auditory, imagistic, and sequential memory become subservient to the eyes. The following techniques will help you build a thorough knowledge of the interrelationship between the melody and the harmonic (chord) changes. By practicing this way, you will develop a mental and physical command of the fingerboard that utilizes your auditory skills (melodic memory), technical skills (dexterity and muscle memory) and theoretical skills (knowledge of all the chord forms and the notes in each key, as well as their intervalic relationships).

1) Memorize the melody first. Later, your goal as an improviser will be to perform an original rendition of the melody, and then be able to dip in and out of it, always hearing it in your inner ear as you improvise over its chord changes.

2) To test your knowledge of the melody, put on the metronome and play the melody, alternating between playing it physically and playing it mentally. In a sense, you will be turning yourself into a human piano roll: you will start playing the melody and suddenly drop out, but hear the melody moving on by using your inner ear; then come back in wherever the melody has moved on to. Each time you play the tune in this way, try to vary where you drop out and where you come back in. This exercise will force you to know how to come in on the melody at any point, which is a skill you need as an improviser.

3) Memorize the root notes of the chords.

4) Play the root notes of the chords on the violin while singing or whistling the melody.

5) Play the 1, 3, 5, 7 (or 1, 3, 5, 6 depending on the chord form) of each chord one note at a time to the metronome so that time sequences and interrelationships are properly programmed into your auditory memory. The following example demonstrates exactly how you would approach this exercise. 🏹

6) Now play the chord tones upside-down: ➤➤

Third to root   5   3   1   etc.

   3, 1

   5, 3, 1

   7, 5, 3, 1

7) Try scrambling the chord tones while playing them in time to the metronome (so that you have to think on a time demand):

   3, 5, 7, 1

   3, 1, 5, 7

   7, 1, 5, 3, and so on

8) If you've successfully completed all of these steps without referring to the printed music, you are ready to go on and practice the corresponding scales for these chord changes. Try to image, or see in your mind's eye, each scale as if it's a blueprint or a map; actually image all of the notes of the chord's corresponding scale simultaneously, the way a pianist can picture playing more than one note at a time. The ability to perceive an entire scale at once provides greater facility during improvisation.

9) Once you've spent some time mentally mapping out the layout of the key on your fingerboard, then actually play each scale in the order it appears in the tune. Make sure you know the names of the notes as you play them. Use the exercises detailed in this next section to deepen your facility with each scale.

INTERVALIC MASTERY OF THE KEYS

If we only wanted to improvise in scale-like runs, then diatonic practice would be adequate. The demands of improvisation, though, necessitate a total command of the fingerboard. Without developing this kind of technical mobility, there is a tendency to cling to the secure and familiar passageways, however limiting. The following practice material is designed to help open up every possible avenue on the fingerboard, until all options are available to your ears, hands, and imagination.

You will notice that the first few exercises are written out in complete form in the key of C. They are designed to cover the full range of the instrument in first position, rather than only moving from tonic (the root note of the key) to its octave. Try to use the notation as a reference only, so that you grasp the concept, turn away from the music stand, and apply it. If you revert to a "follow-the-dots" approach, you won't get as much out of these exercises. For this reason, I've only written out two's (seconds with a jump of a third), three's (groups of three with a jump of a fourth), thirds, and waterfall scales. Use the other intervals suggested to develop your own patterns.

Once you've mastered these exercises in the key of C, apply them to any key or scale-type that you are currently interested in learning. Also be sure to refer to the various rhythms available for use on these patterns, so that you work on dexterity and speed simultaneously.

Rhythms
Apply these rhythms to each of the patterns outlined

Pattern 1: Two's

IMPROVISING VIOLIN

Pattern II: Three's

Pattern III: Thirds (single direction)

Pattern IV: Thirds (single direction)

Pattern V: Thirds (mixed direction)

Pattern VI: Thirds (mixed direction)

Pattern VII: Waterfall Scales

Four Patterns Using 1 3 5's

Two Patterns Using Perfect Fourths

Using any of the intervals outlined below, you can create a number of practice patterns to help you develop your facility on any scale you are currently working on.

Intervals

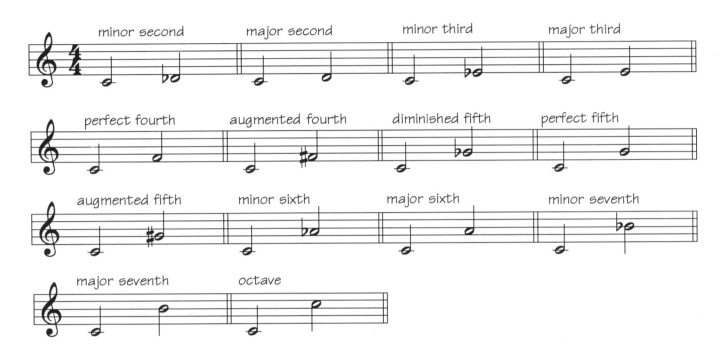

THE JAZZ MODES

Every once in a while, you will come across a tune that does not base its improvisation on chord changes. There may very well be chords written in for the accompaniment of the melody, but when it comes time to solo, it will say something like: "Solo in D Dorian."

In jazz, there are a group of seven scales, called "modes." Some of the modes correspond to chordal scales, and some don't. It's helpful to learn these scales because they are all derived from the major scale. For instance, you can find the dorian mode by starting on the second tone of C major,

and moving to its ninth. If you wish to apply the dorian mode to another tonal center, simply follow the model of whole and half steps.

Soloing off a single scale offers a different type of challenge from soloing off of chord changes. In this case, you have to create a totally interesting and eventful solo only using seven notes. The thirty-two bar format doesn't usually apply to this type of music (although you can find it in some tunes, like "So What" by Miles Davis).

THE JAZZ MODES

Ionian: the same as a major scale

1 2 3 4 5 6 7

Dorian: the same as a minor seventh scale (-7)
or refer back a whole step to find the major scale equivalent

1 2 b3 4 5 6 b7

Phrygian: refer back a third to
find the major scale equivalent

1 b2 b3 4 5 b6 b7

Lydian: the same as a Maj(#11) or refer back a
fourth to find the major scale equivalent

1 2 3 #4 5 6 7

Mixolydian: the same as a dominant seventh (7)
or refer back a fifth to find the major scale equivalent

1 2 3 4 5 6 b7

Aeolian: the same as a natural minor scale or refer back
a sixth or up a minor third to find the major scale equivalent

1 2 b3 4 5 b6 b7

Locrian: the same as a half diminished scale or go
up a half step to find its major scale equivalent

1 b2 b3 4 b5 b6 b7

IMPROVISING VIOLIN

Even though this book offers a number of exercises for you to use to develop mastery over the technical and theoretical aspects of improvisation, I want to take a moment and emphasize the more musical and imaginative side of development.

Nothing can replace the aural process; this is how you learned to speak as a child. Listen to improvising musicians as often as you can, whether recorded or live. Even study their solos by learning them note for note—first vocally, and then on the violin. This is not for the sake of imitation; it is for the purpose of learning how advanced improvisers hear, phrase, interpret, thread from chord change to change, and so on. When you select a tune to learn, listen to as many recorded examples of the tune as you can to reinforce your auditory memory of the melody and harmony (chord changes). Hearing what other artists have created on those changes can also give you a sense of rhythmic and improvisational sound possibilities that might not occur to you otherwise.

Secondly, give yourself time to just freely investigate sounds on your violin without thinking about a specific tune. For instance:

• Explore as many textural sounds as you can possibly find. Start with your bowing arm by experimenting with the juxtaposition of pressure from the index finger (or from releasing arm weight into gravity) with bow speed, and amount of hair used. Come up with as many different sounds as you can. Then switch to your left hand: try different combinations of speed and pressure for finger to finger motion; experiment with various types of slides (see the unit *Blues Fiddle*). Now combine right- and left-hand discoveries.

• Choose a key and a scale type (this could be based on one of the chordal scales you might have encountered in a tune you are learning) or mode, and create a lengthy improvisation (twenty to thirty minutes) using that scale. Each time you hit a plateau and start to feel bored, if you stay with it, you will discover new ideas.

• Now try the opposite: a series of one-minute improvisations. This is also an extremely effective approach to developing improvisatory skills. While doing a live radio show in California, pianist Allaudine Mathieu suggested that we play one-minute improvisations. It's amazing how our sense of structural integrity was stimulated by having to create a cohesive musical idea that had a beginning, middle, and an end, in just sixty seconds!

• Try creating an improvisation as if you are telling a story. This will help you to be in the moment while simultaneously working with the solo as a whole, integrated fabric. In fact, when studying with Bobby McFerrin, one of the most important ideas he introduced was that of not changing one's idea on every "breath." Thinking/listening for a cohesive line is the glue that binds all of the disparate elements—tone, pitch, technique, melody, and chord changes—into one complete "story."

This first exercise is designed to help you move fluidly through all twelve keys, while retaining a melodic line in your auditory memory.

Let's use an excerpt from a solo created by saxophonist Lester Young, which was recorded in 1939. The exercises that we use on this solo can be applied to any excerpt from a solo or melodic pattern.

Begin by playing the following line until you know its sound well enough to be able to whistle or hum it **without** looking at the sheet music. Familiarize yourself with its internal structure: What are the intervals being used? What key is this line in, and when is the tonic stated? If there are intervals that you aren't familiar with, isolate and practice them in an ascending and descending motion.

Now transpose the line into each of the twelve keys moving up chromatically. There are several ways to approach transposition. One is entirely by ear, without even knowing what notes you are playing, what key you're in, or what the intervalic relationships are. The other method is to become sharply

aware of the internal structural relationships. For instance, in this line, there is a perfect fourth between the last note of the line and the first note in the new key when moving upward chromatically. Awareness of this relationship can dramatically increase your ease in transposition.

Continue to move up chromatically...

Now that you've played the line in all twelve keys, you can play some games with it to increase your technique and knowledge of the fingerboard. Play the line with the met-ronome at 60 and put it into 5/4 time. Every other key will start on the downbeat (on the tick).

Continue to move up chromatically...

Try doubling or tripling each note. Use short strokes and keep your right hand relaxed.

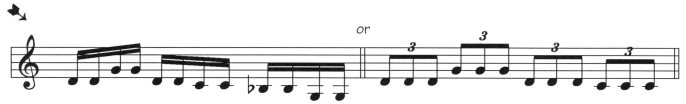

You can add an extra note above or below each note of the line. Choose a specific interval and use it consistently.

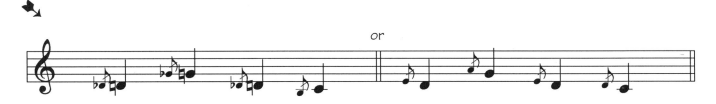

Now play the line up and down chromatically, staying on the G and D strings and shifting up the fingerboard one position at a time. Repeat this process an octave higher.

Continue to move up chromatically using this fingering...

Using each of the exercises listed above, gradually increase the speed on the metronome, notch by notch, until you are playing the line at a fast tempo. Move ahead only when you have mastered the line at your present speed. The criteria for mastery should include: playing in tune, <u>knowing where you are at all times</u> (the key and the names of the notes as you play them), good tone, and relaxed hands.

Up until now, we've only been moving the line chromatically. To really give yourself a challenge, you can try moving the line through other intervalic cycles. To start with, move the line in minor thirds. In order to prevent repetition of the same four keys, you will need to dip back a half step every four keys:

Continue to move up
in minor thirds...

Let's take a new melodic line and move it in descending fifths. In this case, the line starts on the fifth of the key. To be able to transpose this successfully, you will have to be able to picture the tonic and the fifth simultaneously. When you finish this exercise, invent some of your own melodic patterns and move them through various intervalic cycles.

Continue to move through
the cycle of fifths...

USING UPPER AND LOWER NEIGHBORING TONES

Here are a series of exercises that will further your knowledge of the chord changes on any given tune as well as help prepare you for the use of bebop passing tones. Set the metronome at a slow tempo and proceed as follows:

1) Choose a tune that you would like to learn or are currently working on.

2) Play the root notes of the chords.

3) Add in the chromatic lower neighbor of each root note.

4) Play the upper scale tone down to the root note.

5) Once you have successfully completed steps one through three, try playing both the lower to the upper to the root.

6) Reverse this process: upper to lower to root.

7) Repeat this entire process using the third of each key, then the fifth, and then the seventh.

The example below applies some of these steps to the first four measures of the Bb blues:

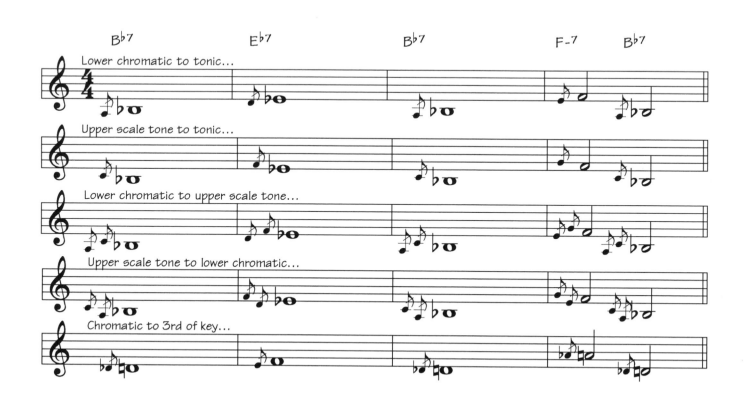

A WORD ABOUT SYNCOPATION AND INFLECTION

Classical players tend to approach their rhythms differently than jazz musicians. For one thing, they tend to be a bit on top of or even a smidgeon ahead of the beat. The rhythms will frequently be more symmetrical, with emphasis landing more often on the strong part of the beat than the weak part. Therefore, it is often difficult for classically trained players to learn how to hang a bit behind the beat, or to use syncopated rhythms (beginning a note on the last half of one beat and holding it through the first half of the next beat). Try using the following techniques to work on your relationship to time:

1) Put the metronome on at 60. Clap with the metronome. If you hear your clap and the tick as two separate sounds—no matter how close—then you are coming in early or late. However, if it suddenly seems as though someone unplugged the metronome, because you only hear your clap, this means that you are coming in exactly on the tick.

2) Practice syncopated rhythms as well as quarter note triplets.

3) Familiarize yourself with placing inflection (light accentuation by using a slight dip in weight with the index finger on the bow) on the weak part of the beat.

4) Put the metronome on and play eighth note passages with the tick sounding on the two and four of the measure. Try rotating accentuation, so that at first you are accenting the first eighth note of the first beat, then the second eighth note of the first beat, then the first eighth note of the second beat, and so on, until you've mastered inflecting each one.

Syncopated rhythms   Quarter-note Triplets   Jazz inflections

In 1937, Joe Venuti wrote a book titled "Violin Rhythm" in which he encouraged aspiring jazz violinists to develop their knowledge of and command over as many rhythmic phrases as possible. Although the book has been out of print for decades, you can follow his example by training your ears and bowing arm to be as fluent, rhythmically speaking, as possible. Use the rhythmic phrases on the following pages to help develop your expertise in this area. Apply them to warm-ups as well as to improvisation.

Rhythmic Studies

IMPROVISING VIOLIN

Most tunes that you learn from sheet music offer little more than the melody and chord changes. Bowings and textural effects are left up to the discretion of the player. Since most violinists come from a more classical orientation toward bowings and left-hand techniques, there will be a tendency to only work with the sounds you are already familiar with. Here are a few textural approaches to the shaping of key notes within the musical phrase:

Slide Technique

There are many ways to slide into a note with the left hand depending upon length of approach and speed of motion, and even these can be more widely varied by the pressure and speed of the bow's movement. If a slide is notated, it will look as follows, but it's up to you to determine the most appropriate style for the slide.

The Smear

Rather than moving from note to note with a clear articulation, one can smear the motion through a slide or by leaning the finger up and back.

Unison Variation

If you decide to repeat the same note a number of times, it can be highly effective to change fingers on each repetition, so that there is a subtle variation of the pitch with each repetition.

Leading Tones

Use the chromatic lower neighbor or scale tone upper neighbor as discussed earlier in this section of the book to color the entry into a note. (Joe Venuti referred to this technique as a "flare.")

The Whip

When moving up into a primary tone, you can roll up through the scale tones as follows.

The Bend

It's nice to put a subtle dip in pitch on a note by leaning the finger back and then quickly returning it to its original position.

The Fall (or spill)

You can fall up or down from a note to an indistinct pitch.

Shakes

Use a wide, hysterical vibrato to color an important note.

Ghost Notes

Ghost notes are created by giving the note its rhythmic value while only subtly implying a definite pitch. The timing and pressure of the bow are crucial to make this work.

Chops

Originally used in bluegrass music, Turtle Island String Quartet popularized this method of playing rhythmic backup on violin in jazz. This percussive effect is created at the frog, and the bow actually angles in towards the bridge as it lands so that the pitch is indeterminable, and the landing is stacatto.

For more textural effects, see the chapter titled "Jazz Violin."

In 1988, Leroy Jenkins invited me to work on a video titled *Improvised Violin: Four Personal Views* which included John Blake, Jr. and Billy Bang. When we shot the video, it was without rehearsal so that our discussions and responses were spontaneous. I remember the group's laughter of recognition when Leroy mentioned that feeling of "scuffling," when his bowing arm would struggle to keep pace with his imagination. We knew the feeling well! Here are a few guidelines you can use to help keep incoordination to a minimum.

Too much bow length

Classical pieces often require strident, long bows, sometimes even on short notes. This doesn't go over well in non-classical playing, which requires a more relaxed sound quality. In addition, many players equate speed with effort and inadvertently use too much bow length, particularly while playing fast. Since the only way to get a quality sound when using too much bow length is to move the bow out over the fingerboard, this offense can be easily detected by the amount of rosin you will find on your fingerboard. As you speed up, use less hair, center the bow between the bridge and the fingerboard, relax more, and try to use the downbow on each string crossing as an opportunity to drop your arm weight into gravity, thereby giving your muscles constant relief. Since muscular contraction hinders movement, this friendly use of gravity will foster greater fluidity of motion.

Improper hand/arm coordination while crossing strings

Some players try to initiate fast movement from the wrist. The wrist muscle is extremely weak compared to the forearm; this makes detailed control much more difficult and can cause problems with carpal tunnel syndrome or tendinitis later. I use two terms to describe the primary movement of the arm during string crossings: *pump* or *pivot*. The note-to-note movement should be a push/pull motion powered by the forearm, while the upper arm acts like a pump — raising and lowering — to move you from string to string. If you're bobbing between the same two strings for an entire passage, though, try placing your upper arm so that your bow is resting on both strings; keep your upper arm fairly still, and pivot your forearm from the elbow. Practice isolating each movement (pump versus pivot) using short repetitive bows to develop control.

Fast Bows

The biceps muscle is its weakest when it is lengthened by playing with a straight arm at the tip of the bow (unless you have an extremely long arm), or when it is shortened by playing too close to the frog. Place the bow where its natural weight can produce a good tone with the least amount of effort, keeping your arm position at a right angle, which will enable you to use the biceps muscle more efficiently.

Jazz Bowings

Since the downbow motion of the bow tends to place a natural accent within the phrase, how and when you slur (combine more than one note in the same bow) can dramatically affect your phrasing. The first three measures of the following example demonstrate a classical approach to bowing eighth notes. It is more appropriate, however, to use the bowing demonstrated in measure four for swing and jazz styles. Apply this bowing first to scales, and then to random improvisations using eighth notes. For further variations on bowing eighth notes, see the chapter titled "Folk Fiddle."

SOME TECHNICAL TIPS

The Violin Position

Some violinists tend to hold their instrument on their chest, rather than on the shoulder. This locks the left elbow into one position reducing the forearm's ability to rotate and line the fingers up in a perpendicular relationship to the fingerboard. The left hand must then work harder to compensate for the lack of flexibility and support from the forearm. The frontal position of the violin can also force the bowing arm too far back by the side, unnecessarily engaging the right shoulder muscle for string crossings.

To position your violin so that it compliments both arms, use a shoulder rest to free the left hand from the responsibility of holding up the fiddle, and to help increase mobility in the left arm. Choose the most comfortable shoulder rest for your body-type by visiting a string shop and trying out their various models. (I particularly recommend Kun or Wolf, because they are adjustable.) Make sure the shoulder rest is seated on your shoulder, not your chest. Your right elbow should be positioned over your right hip bone when you bow. Turn your head halfway to the left, lower your chin, and the chin-rest should be there to receive you. If it isn't, something is wrong with the position of the instrument.

The transition from practicing at home to playing with a rhythm section (which usually consists of bass, drums, and either piano or guitar or both) can sometimes be a difficult one. The most common obstacles that deter individuals from playing with other musicians range from fear of not being ready or not being good enough to just simply not knowing how to find other musicians with a common interest in jamming or forming a band.

No amount of practice at home, however, can replace the dynamics that arise when playing with other musicians. You must learn how to interact with others such that you ensemble rhythmically as well as dynamically. The exchange of ideas, as well as the development of a special sensitivity to blending with others are important to your artistic development.

The best attitude to take is to simply accept the fact that you may never feel ready or "good enough" so you may as well not use that as criteria for getting started. In fact, the sooner you begin to play with other musicians on a regular basis, the faster you will progress. Newspaper ads, word of mouth, or signs on bulletin boards at universities, musician's unions, or apartment buildings, are all methods my students have used to successfully connect with other musicians. The worst that can happen is that you can get together with someone who isn't on the same level, realize the mistake, and move on to finding someone who is.

Some of the skills you will need to develop in order to play with other musicians, will include kicking the tune off at the correct tempo, trading fours, choosing a repertoire, and so on.

Tempo

Choosing the correct tempo for a tune and counting it off to get the tune started is simple enough. The main task here is to be able to hear the tune in your head and not count it off at the wrong tempo. Many musicians often count off a tune too fast for the group's ability to hold it together or compose interesting solos without straining.

Trading Fours

Ordinarily, each musician will take a solo that lasts anywhere from one to three choruses (although if you feel comfortable enough with the other musicians, you may as well play longer for the practice). Sometimes, however, you will want to trade with the drummer or the bass player. In that case, each solo instrumentalist will take a turn at alternating playing for four bars with, let's say the drummer. For instance: violin—four bars, drums—four bars, saxophone—four bars, drums—four bars, piano—four bars, drums—four bars, and so on. It's also fun to trade two's or even single bars. Really try to "play ball." This means that instead of focusing exclusively on your own ideas, you truly listen to the soloist preceding you and pick up where he or she leaves off.

Listening

It's tempting to stay in one's own head when playing with others. After all, you've spent hundreds if not thousands of hours practicing alone, and you feel comfortable with a certain way of listening and playing. But to truly ensemble with other musicians, you must open your ears to a new level. Don't regard the rhythm section solely as a backdrop to your solo. Try to interact melodically and dynamically. Never listen so much to yourself that you've lost awareness of what the other musicians are playing.

Volume

It's common for violinists to have volume problems when playing with a rhythm section. Try to work out your amplification system before you start jamming with others so that you don't end up bearing down muscularly to be heard. Read the amplification chapter in this book for ideas on how to proceed.

FIRST AMERICAN JAZZ STRING SUMMIT (1984)

AMPLIFICATION

With all of the stylistic exploration taking place on the violin today, there has been an increasing demand on violin makers for an instrument that is capable of greater sound possibilities. Considering the fact that half a century ago, Stuff Smith had to give up performing in Jelly Roll Morton's group because he couldn't be heard above the horns, we've come a long way in the field of amplification. Numerous versions of electric violins have emerged since the forties so that the violin could be heard in blues, jazz, and rock bands; one of the earliest versions included a kind of a megaphone built onto the face of the violin to help amplify the sound! Fortunately, though, the technology has become more sophisticated with each decade.

One of the unspoken jokes shared by professional improvising violinists, is the high percentage of our earned income we've spent on trying out each new product available for amplification. Since our evolution has paralleled the technological development, many of us have purchased each product as it's emerged, resulting in a collection of disasters, ineffectual piles of wires and pickups, and strange-looking and often useless versions of electric violins that gather dust in our closets. Young players today are at an advantage. There is now a wide range of excellent products to choose from. Yet, the challenge still lies in selecting the appropriate device.

The three standard approaches to amplification consist of playing into a microphone, using a pickup—which attaches to the bridge or soundpost—or playing on a solid-body electric violin, which has no acoustic sound and must be plugged into an amp in order to be heard. A pre-amp, an amp, and electronic effects (discussed below) will also be necessary tools for expanding your sound possibilities.

To determine which type of amplification is most suitable to your needs, start by answering these two questions:

1) Is it important to you to maintain, but boost your acoustic sound? If the answer is yes, make sure that this choice is practical to the playing situation. In other words, if you are playing with a large horn section, this may not be the best solution, because the timbre of the amplified acoustic violin probably won't be able to compete. If the answer is no, and you're looking for amplification as well as an electric sound, then you will be dealing with a higher price range ($750 - $3,500), and researching a solid-body violin.

2) What is your budget? Since you can purchase pickups ranging in price from $50 to $500, you will tend to want to base your decision on your spending power. But try not to let money be the governing factor. If you want to use this system for a solid amount of time, you want to sound your best, and you're certain that this is definitely an item you need (rather than something you just want to toy with), it might be worth saving your money and waiting until you can invest in the device that will really be the best solution for you.

Now let's look at each of the amplification components in greater detail.

THE MICROPHONE

A microphone is good for work with small acoustic ensembles requiring light amplification and is one of the best options for maintaining an acoustic sound. Since the mike is stationery, however, it seriously restricts physical mobility (unless it's a small remote mike attached to your tailpiece, like the Crown omni-condenser mike or the Audio Technica ATM35 clip-on mike). There is a limited amount of power the violin can gain through a mike. For large ensembles, the instrument probably won't carry, and players often end up straining in order to be heard, which impairs their ability to play fast or feel comfortable.

Besides the fact that the mike is too far from the instrument to pick up every detail of sound or the full resonance beyond a certain volume level, problems occur with regenerative feedback. This is when, at the speed of sound, the violin is bombarded by the same pulse frequencies it is making. The violin sends these sound pulses out through the mike into the amp, and subsequently the speakers, which then bounce the signal right back into the resonant wood of the violin, in a self-feeding cycle. This causes the unpleasant sound we call feedback.

If using a mike is the most appropriate solution for you, make sure that you request a goose-neck or boom-stand; either will give you greater flexibility. Raise the stand as high as you can and then position the mike so that it's aimed above your right F-hole. This position will prevent the possibility of hitting the stand with your bowing arm, and give the most direct connection between the resonance of your sound—which occurs in the body of the instrument before its departure through the F-holes—and the mike.

THE PICKUP

Even if you use an excellent microphone and sound system, it is extremely difficult to match the timbre of a solid-body guitar, brass ensemble, or full rhythm section. The violin simply can't cut through. To even begin to compete, it is necessary to use a pickup.

A pickup is a small device that usually attaches to the bridge (except the Kurmann soundpost system, which attaches to the soundpost). It is fairly easy to install or remove, but some of the systems available leave your bridge sticky or gooey. This leftover residue will impair your acoustic sound. If you buy a bridge with an already built-in pickup, you won't have to worry about installation or removal, but you will have to have the bridge carved to fit your instrument (except the Zeta bridge), and the acoustic sound might not be as good as with a regular bridge.

How the Pickup Works

A pickup is actually a transducer; it catches sound vibrations as they move from the strings into the bridge. The pickup immediately translates these sound waves into an electronic signal. While the acoustic violin relies on the bridge, sound post, and body of the instrument for tone, the pickup bypasses all of this. For this reason, poor tone is a common problem for amplified string instruments unless the pickup has built-in equalization for each of the four strings. Another solution is to use a pre-amp with a built-in equalizer to boost volume and control its frequencies (treble, mid-range, and bass). Just make sure the pre-amp was designed to be compatible with your pickup. The pre-amp is then plugged into the amp.

What To Look For in A Pickup

It's better to spend a little more and buy a pickup system that:

1) has built-in equalization or a companion equalization box;

2) is either permanently installed so that you don't have to constantly mount and then remove it, or that installs without a mess.

The Fishman V-200 Violin Transducer attaches to one wing of the bridge with a clever spring device and has a nice smooth, present sound. The extremely small size and light weight minimizes any damping or muting of the natural bridge action, and installation is quick and easy. In addition, one can purchase the Fishman PRO-EQ pre-amp, which is a compact and portable equalizer developed to complement the pickup system. The PRO-EQ gives control over bass, mid-range, treble, and brilliance. Fishman has also combined its transducer with a Crown mike (V-200-M). This system works best through their Blender pre-amp, which gives separate controls for both the transducer and the mike.

The L.R. Baggs Violin Pickup contains a miniature three dimensional sensor built into a bridge that must be mounted on your violin. The companion Para Acoustic D.I. direct box contains a preamp and equalizer which provides greater tone control. The amplified sound is rich and strong. Once you

FISHMAN V-200

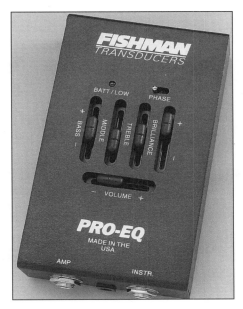

FISHMAN PRO-EQ

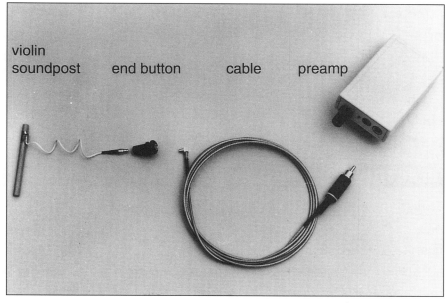

violin
soundpost   end button   cable   preamp

KURMANN SOUNDPOST SYSTEM

install the bridge on your favorite acoustic violin, however, you will alter its acoustic sound. Better to use a second violin.

The Kurmann soundpost system is built into the sound post, and needs to be installed by a violin repairman. Once installed, it remains there for the duration, makes a wonderfully balanced amplified sound, and does not alter the regular acoustic tone of the instrument. The wire runs back through the end button, so that it's not in your way, and the system comes with a pre-amp that has adjustable equalization included. One of the advantages of this system, is the fact that it is extremely good for recording, which is not the case with most other pickups. The player can plug directly into the board (line-in) from the pickup and produce excellent tonal clarity.

The Barbera bridge has a separate pickup for each string, making it extremely sensitive to the full range of tonal color, Like the Baggs system, the bridge does alter the

acoustic sound of the instrument. It might be better to own two violins, so that you still have an acoustic instrument to practice on.

The Zeta Retro Pak offers another alternative. It includes a bridge/pickup assembly, tailpiece with fine tuners, pre-amp, and 5" cable. The sound quality is warm, clear, and

ZETA RETRO PAK

consistent, but the violin won't yield much of an acoustic sound once it is installed. The Zeta Retro Pak creates an affordable electric alternative to buying a solid-body violin. The pickup system has MIDI capabilities, as well. MIDI is an acronym for Musical Instrument Digital Interface. This means that the bridge can be used in tandem with a computer music program or the Zeta MIDI system. Zeta also has the Strados VS-104 pickup. This pickup system uses two piezo pickups per string. The design is so unique that feedback is impossible. Bridge, tailpiece and a 20-foot cable are included.

ELECTRIC SOLID-BODY VIOLINS

The electromagnetic pickup commonly used on solid-body guitars differs from the transducer in that rather than responding to sound vibrations, it responds to movement within a magnetic field. This means the movement of the metal strings creates the signal. The electromagnetic pickup works poorly on a traditional violin because the wood and shape of the instrument act as a medium or catchall for any electric movement in the room, particularly that of other electric instruments. This results in hum, distortion, and/or feedback. Thus, a solid- body violin is necessary.

Since electric instruments do not rely on hollow sound chambers, there is no reason to maintain the traditional shape of the violin. This gives electric violin designers more leeway to be creative with the look of the instrument. The most important factor to be aware of when shopping for an electric violin besides the tone is the feel of the instrument. Some of the instruments on the market are heavy or awkward to hold; others have slightly different measurements (the length from chin to bridge may differ). This can be extremely uncomfortable for a player who has spent thousands of hours training on an acoustic violin. Do not purchase an instrument without playing on it for at least an hour! If your arms become tired, or you feel at all uncomfortable, don't buy it, or you may be setting yourself up for muscular injury down line.

Darol Anger

I've been working with a company called Zeta Violins, and they've actually produced a violin that will control any synthesizer. And that's very exciting for me because I can get a lot of different kinds of sounds out of the instrument, even more kinds of sounds than I've been able to get out of an acoustic. And, it's really wonderful to suddenly become a flute, or a horn, or a drum, or even a large orchestral string section. It's really exciting to play the violin and have 40 violins come out.

There are a few excellent, solid-body electric violins available on the market today. Zeta's two models, Quartet and Mark O'Connor Signature Series, have MIDI capability and though expensive are state-of-the-art machines. They yield the same warm, clear, consistent signature tone (without feedback) that Zeta has become famous for. In addition, they are ergonomi-

ZETA QUARTET AND STRADOS VIOLINS

tions available) instrument called "The Viper Violin." The Viper is rigged with frets, enabling the player to access two- and three-note chords like a guitar, without compromising the beautiful subtleties of an acoustic violin fingerboard, although for those who prefer it, a fretless version is available. The instrument comes with a chest support system, which eliminates the need for a chin rest and shoulder pad. The Viper, when played through an amp cleanly (without distortion) can sound like a cello, viola and violin all in one. With distortion and frets, it can sound like an electric guitar.

cally designed so that the player is assured of a high level of physical comfort while playing, and give the option of either four or five strings. Zeta also offers The Strados, an affordable alternative, without MIDI, that gives violinists the ability to successfully produce the sound of an acoustic violin at necessary stage volumes without feedback.

The T.F. Barrett line includes four-, five-, and six-string violins; the instruments use the Barbera Transducer pickup. Their tonal character is a nice blend between acoustic and electric. Barbera's transducer pickup is also used by Jensen, who is another electric violin maker. And, if you want to really rock out, then check out Mark Wood's line of rock violins.

Mark Wood is a rock violinist who, after ten years of research and development, created a six-string (with four and five-string op-

THE VIPER

The Pre-Amp

With today's systems, a pre-amp (which you plug your violin into) is not absolutely necessary, but can give an extra boost to your volume, and also supplies you with close-at-hand control of the equalization (treble and bass ratios). Note, that some of the pickup systems discussed above, come with their own companion pre-amp.

The Amp

The amp is a separate (and usually large) unit containing built-in speakers. The input, whether from a pickup or a microphone, is magnified and fed through the speakers. Some amps have tone controls. Really good amps have built-in equalizers. Purchasing decisions should be based on budget, volume requirements, the tone (some amps add warmth, and some yield a more metallic, rock type of sound), and transportation facilities. If you want a small boost in volume, a lightweight small frame, and the option of playing out of doors without electricity, the mouse amp is an excellent solution, though it isn't the best sounding amp to use because of its size. Most amps offer the option of reverb, which can add a nice ambient quality to your sound.

Originally, the frequency response of amps were designed for instruments like electric guitar and bass. This rendered them incapable of carrying the full tonal range of the amplified violin. It's only been in the last few years that music companies have begun to manufacture amps designed specifically for the range required by acoustic instruments. The Fishman Acoustic Performer Pro is a good example of this new trend. Its high frequency drivers, ambient on-instrument digital reverb, and multiple inputs (so that a pickup and mike can be plugged in simultaneously and send both signals in a balanced manner) make it capable of handling and enhancing anything the violin is capable of sending.

When you're ready to buy an amp, make sure you test it in the store using your own violin with the pickup system you've selected, so that you get a true representation of the final sound. It's worth it to spend a few more bucks and get an amp that you can live with happily for many years.

Electronic Effects

Electronic effects are gadgets that you can plug into to change your overall sound. *Digital delay*, which creates an echo, *phase shifter*, which fattens the sound and gives it a spatial quality, *octaver*, which adds a second interval (usually an octave, though it can be tuned to any other interval), are just a few of the effects available in either a small box, or rack-mountable size. Rock violinist Mark Wood recommends the Zoom box, which is a small box that you plug into. It offers a wide range of effects to choose from.

The most difficult aspect of working with extra effects is the expense. To make sure that you don't invest in something that you may not like, try borrowing it from a friend, or go to the local music store and try it out there.

The Use of Fine Tuners

For centuries, classical violinists have used their pegs to tune their strings. An attitude bordering on snobbery has developed against the use of fine tuners, which are viewed as inferior. Besides the fact that well-fitted pegs are generally not always a luxury found on instruments in a $2,500

(and under) range, fine tuners are a must when it comes to playing on an amplified instrument.

Since it isn't possible to tune quietly when one's sound is blasting through speakers, the use of fine tuners for each of the four strings is an excellent way to make fast, subtle adjustments. Try to avoid the use of E fine tuners for the four strings since they often don't accommodate thicker strings and tend to break more quickly. Use the Thomastik tailpiece (or a comparable model) with four built-in fine tuners instead.

SUPPORT MATERIALS

Mark Wood: 516-767-7084
Mark Wood Productions, P.O. Box 2074, Port Washington, NY 11050

The Kurmann Soundpost: 201-839-0196
c/o Skyline Guitars, 401 Skyline Lakes Dr., Ringwood, N.J. 07456

Fishman: 1-800-FISHMAN
340-D Fordham Road, Wilmington, MA 01887

Zeta Music Systems: 1-800-622-6434
2230 Livingston Street, Oakland, CA 94606

Richard Barbera: 718-816-3025
21 Louis Street, Staten Island, NY 10304

L.R. Baggs: 805-929-3545
483 North Frontage Road, Nipomo, CA 93444

INTRODUCTION TO THE STYLISTIC UNITS

Certain elements of blues, swing, rock, and jazz technique are similar on the violin. Even if you are only interested in one or two of these styles, please make sure that you take the time to read through the section titled "Technique" in all of the chapters, as each section offers valuable stylistic tips that may be intertwinable.

MUSIC MINUS ONE

When learning to improvise on a new tune or stylistic structure (such as the blues), it's important to hear the chord changes from an external source while strengthening your inner ear and knowledge of the melody and chords. Since most of us don't have another musician or rhythm section we can call in every time we practice, it's best to use "Music Minus One" recordings. These are prerecorded rhythm sections that supply the accompaniment for the music we are learning. If you play a wrong note or get lost in the structure, the rhythm section is always there to set you back on course. I will be recommending specific recordings (available on CD, cassette, or record) from Jamey Aebersold's Jazz Aids series at the back of each chapter. Occasionally, if available, I will also recommend Music Minus One materials from other companies. Check at the back of each chapter for order information on these materials.

LEARNING TO IMPROVISE

The method you use to learn something new has everything to do with how fast and how well you will master the information. Before we launch into the specific styles together, please take a look at the following suggested approach to learning to improvise within a blues or jazz structure (also refer back to the "Building Foundation" section):

1) Start by memorizing the root notes (for instance, the root note for a C7 chord is C) of the chords.

2) Using a metronome or recorded accompaniment, hold the root note to each chord for the designated number of beats. For instance, in the country blues, you would hold a C for four bars (measures), an F for two bars, and so on.

3) Now try playing the root note and its third; for instance, if it's a C7 chord, you would play a C and an E.

4) If you are playing the root and third by memory, add the fifth in, so that you are playing the 1, 3, and 5.

5) Then add the 7th: 1 3 5 7

6) To test your knowledge of the chord changes, turn the chord tones upside down: play the third to the root, the 5 3 1 and then the 7 5 3 1.

7) Now review the scales that correspond to each of the chords: for instance, a C7 scale is a C major scale with a flatted seventh. (See "Building A Foundation")

8) Sing the root notes as you name the chords from memory in time to a metronome or accompaniment.

9) Now you are ready to start to improvise. Your improvisation will follow the chord changes, so that the notes you work with for each measure will be dictated by when each chord takes place and how long it lasts.

THE CREATIVE MUSE

Even after you've practiced scales and patterns in all twelve keys, studied the chords, and mastered the chordal scales, you may find yourself saying, "Now what do I do?" or "How do I apply this to improvisation?" The answer is "slowly." Learning to improvise on a jazz tune takes time. This book can only hope to give you an overview of some of the components and steps involved. Often, a really facile and skilled improvisation on a given tune can take years to develop. But every step of the way will expand your ability and is worth the challenge.

Many musicians go through an awkward period of time when dealing with chord changes for the first time. They often feel like their creativity has been submerged. Improvisation over chord changes is a whole-brain activity. The left brain is engaged in remembering the names of the chords in their proper order, and the names of the notes in each scale, while the right brain is imaging the placement of those notes on the fingerboard, and creating fresh, new musical ideas.

If you have not developed all of these skills equally, there will be a difficult phase during which you will be strenghthening your weak areas. Once this has been accomplished, you will be able to achieve balance. Sometimes this process occurs over a long period of time. Don't be discouraged. Take note of your strengths and weaknesses and do everything you can to build the weak areas as quickly as possible.

If you are not experienced at working with chord changes, always follow an intense session of heavy focus on the chords by giving yourself free reign. Pick up your instrument and play freely and expressively for a good half hour or so, without thinking at all. Then come back into the work and smoke your brain some more!

BLUES FIDDLE

The blues. It's a tremendously rich and expressive music, simple in form, yet capable of creating worlds of color, texture, and feeling. As we discussed earlier, it is little known that the two primary instruments involved in creating the blues back in the 1700s were voice and violin! This is probably because the violin lends itself naturally to the vocal quality of the blues. Both voice and violin can slide into notes, tumble effortlessly through semi-tones, tease and tickle the ears, howling one moment and whispering the next.

The violin can be used in the blues to state or mirror the melody, to play fillers between vocal lines, and as an active solo instrument within the arrangement of the song.

Playing a blues melody requires fluidity, expressiveness, and the ability to go beyond the "composed" notes, putting more of your own individual sound and feel into the music. One note played with tremendous expression can have more power than a cascade of fancy sixteenth notes executed perfectly but without involvement.

A bluesy sound on fiddle comes from incorporating different types of slides, vibrato, and bow inflection into an improvisation that is based upon notes that comply with the chord changes. Let's take a more in-depth, hands-on look at the two major areas of skill important to playing blues on the violin: technique and structure.

BLUES TECHNIQUE

Vibrato

In blues (and jazz), vibrato is a seasoning. It is rarely used the same way on every note; variety of expression is created through using different types of vibrato. The two variables involved—width and speed—can be altered and combined in a number of ways. For instance, try moving slowly in and out of a pitch with a wide roll, or rolling evenly while covering a smaller circumference.

Here is an exercise to help you gain control over the speed and width of your roll. Make sure that you keep your thumb relaxed, your wrist straight, and your finger pressure light.

In third position, place your second finger on an E on the A string. Put the metronome on at 80, and start with a wide quarter note roll. Rolling a quarter tone under the pitch and back up to it (the open E string will ring in sympathy each time you roll back up to the E note), try to keep your hand parallel to the fingerboard and don't lean your palm on the instrument. If all goes well, try an eighth note roll, and then a sixteenth note roll. As you go faster, reduce the width of motion and stay relaxed.

As you practice with each of your four fingers, always use an E note to ensure that you don't go out of tune.

Blues Slides

A blues slide can cover a slight distance moving quickly into the desired pitch, or it can tease or ooze its way into the note from above or below the desired pitch. Here, the main variables are distance and speed. It is difficult, however, to achieve a fluid slide if you place too much vertical pressure down into the fingerboard, or if you hold onto the violin with a great deal of tension. A good slide comes from a relaxed hold, and minimum pressure from the moving finger.

Bow Pressure

You can develop a variety of sounds by allowing your bow's pressure on the string to change. Experiment with pressure, speed and amount of bow length. When you pull the bow quickly with a light pressure, covering, let's say, one-third of the bow—all the while sliding up into a note—you'll get a very different sound from what you'd get if you were to slide into that same note while applying the same pressure and moving the bow slowly. It's this variety that will add color, texture, and expression to your sound.

BLUES STRUCTURE

The blues form consists of twelve bars. Although there are several different types of chord progressions for the blues, once you've mastered the structure for each, that same structure can be transferred to any of the twelve keys. The country blues, which is the simplest version, consists of three chords: I, IV, and V. For instance, if you're playing in the key of G, they would be G, C, and D. Jazz blues is generally more complex, but the additional chords found in this style are simply added to the ones you would have already learned for the country blues. If you think of it in an historical context, after the blues had been around for a while, and there were thousands of tunes written on the same simple structure, musicians wanted more of a challenge, and greater harmonic complexity, so they added in extra chords.

For instance, in the country blues form, the first four measures usually consist of one chord. But in the jazz blues form, while that one chord will be primary to the opening four measures, there will be other chords added in to create a more sophisticated harmonic progression. For this reason, I encourage you to start with the simpler blues form, the country blues, and master it in all twelve keys, before moving on to the jazz blues form. If you truly learn the chord changes by examining the structure rather than memorizing each separate chord, it will be easy to apply that structure to the twelve keys.

Scales in the Blues

While a seven-note scale is fine to use in the blues, the most popular scale is the pentatonic (five-note) scale. See the "Rock Violin" chapter for a number of pentatonic exercises designed to help you develop facility in all twelve keys. There are two extra notes available to use in either a pentatonic or diatonic scale. You can flat the third or the fifth tones in the scale in addition to using these notes in their natural positions.

Bb blues scale   Blues scale with additional blue notes   Pentatonic blues scale

Bb Country Blues

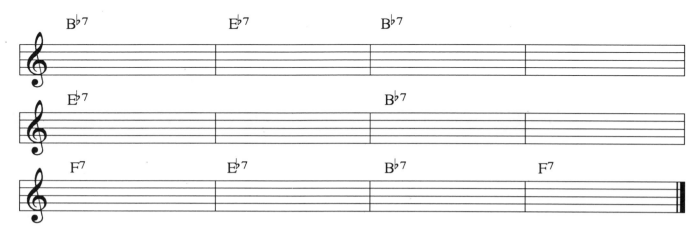

Bb Jazz Blues

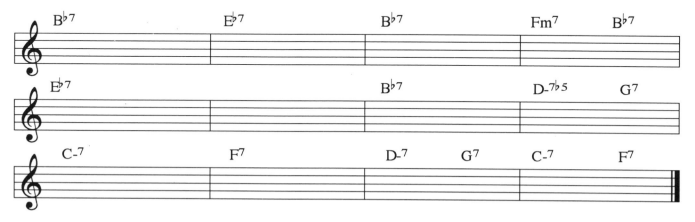

While music notation can't possible capture the way that Claude Williams swings, squeezes, and rolls his notes, you can certainly gain a great deal through studying his solos for cohesive form and for the creative melodic phrases that he builds over the chord changes. Notice how he takes an opening theme and repeats it with a small change. Then, in measure three, he uses the Eb as a pedal point to counterbalance his rising chromatic line. He continues to use repetition with variation in order to build the solo, and then brings it all back home, just like telling a story.

Whose Blues
(in the style of Claude Williams)

Blues Solo in Bb

IMPROVISING VIOLIN

SUPPORT MATERIALS

Audio/Visual

Blues in All Twelve Keys (Music Minus One): Jazz Aids

Minor Blues in all Twelve Keys (Music Minus One): Jazz Aids

Nothing But the Blues (Music Minus One): Jazz Aids

Blues, Texas Swing (cassette): ProLicks

Improvising Violin, Tape II (cassette series): Homespun Tapes

Recommended Reading

For an in-depth resource on fiddling the blues,
consult my book, *Blues Fiddle* (Oak Publications)

Recommended Listening

B.B. King

Clarence Gatemouth Brown, Claude Williams, Papa John Creach,
Randy Sabien, and Sugarcane Harris(see Discography)

Blues Fiddle (Part I of The Talking Violin): Improvised Music Collective

Reference Contact List

Jazz Aids 1-800-456-1388
c/o Jamey Aebersold, P.O. Box 1244C, New Albany, IN 47151

Homespun Tapes, 1-800-33-TAPES, P.O. Box 694, Woodstock, N.Y. 12498

ProLicks, P.O. Box 31729, Seattle, WA 98103

Improvised Music Collective, P.O. Box 495, NY, NY 10024

Oak Publications, 1-800-431-7187, c/o Music Sales, 5 Bellvale Rd., Chester, NY 10918

SWING VIOLIN

Swing developed after the blues and has a slightly more complex chordal structure. The two most distinctive elements of this up-beat music are actually found in its rhythmic components. The emphasis within the four-beat measure is on the two and four, and improvisation, though it can include any type of rhythmic figure, is predominantly comprised of swinging 8th notes.

Swing violin is probably one of the hardest styles for classical players to adapt to!

Many classical violinists try to swing by playing dotted eighth notes. Literally speaking, the swing rhythm is actually created by tying two eighth-note triplets and playing the third triplet separately. If you approach the swing rhythm with too much analysis, however, you will tend to sound mechanical or stiff. To create a hot, fluid swing rhythm, listen to swing players like Eddie South, Stuff Smith, Joe Venuti, and Stephanne Grapelli as much as you can.

SWING TECHNIQUE

Here are some preparatory exercises you can use to begin to develop this style:

1) To get the feel of the swing pulse, try counting 1 2 3 4 with an emphasis on the 1 while clapping only on the 2nd and 4th beats.

2) To practice swinging your eighth notes, play them incorrectly first, and then correctly.

Incorrect   Correct

3) Apply the following bowing pattern to a two- or three-octave scale. Then try improvising in that key using run-on eighth notes. Notice how this bowing emphasizes inflection (natural accentuation through a change in bow direction) on the weak part of the beat. (See "Folk Fiddle" for additional useful bowings.)

4) Imagining that you are in 4/4 time, set your metronome at 60, so that it is only ticking twice per measure on the 2nd and 4th beats. Start by playing eighth notes on an open string, emphasizing the first note of every measure (the one that corresponds to beat #1). Then try improvising on a scale that you know well, using eighth notes. If you are able to accentuate the first note of each measure while keeping the tick on the 2 and 4, then try playing a scale, a tune, or an improvisation using the same rhythmic emphasis. You will probably gravitate toward playing with the tick sounding on the 1 and 3 of the measure, but just keep trying until it feels natural.

5) Try using the Jazz Aids recording *I Got Rhythm* (Volume 47) to build up your improvisatory abilities in this style. The rhythm section (piano, bass, drums) will give you excellent rhythmic support to master the swing sound.

SWING STRUCTURE

Swing music is built on a 32-bar form. The structure is divided as follows: **A A B A**

Each section is made up of 8 measures. Most of the earlier swing players used a sweet, classical vibrato when playing swing, but it isn't a necessary ingredient. The following swing progression is a fairly typical one.

To begin with, scan the A section and try to analyze why you could successfully use a Bb major scale (with an additional b3, b5, and b7 as passing tones) for your improvisation

throughout this section while happily ignoring the chord changes!

Next, apply the procedure outlined in "Introduction To The Stylistic Units" to master the chord changes in the bridge (B section).

When you are ready to improvise on this structure, start by creating an improvisation using half notes to give yourself a chance to create a well architected line. Then move on to quarter note, eighth note, triplet, sixteenth note, and mixed rhythm improvisations.

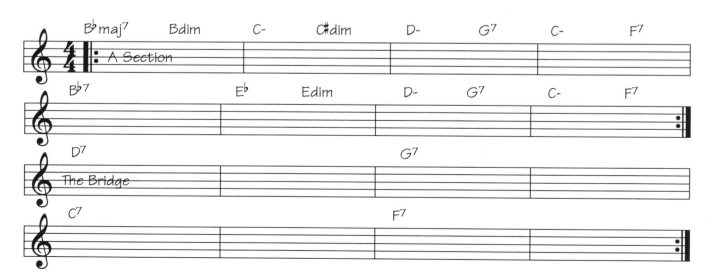

The following is a transcription from jazz violinist Claude William's solo on a popular jazz tune. It can be found on his recording SUMMIT '88 (Huiksi Music). Listen to his playing style on record to supplement this transcription.

IMPROVISING VIOLIN

Lady Swing is a notated solo that has been written over the chord changes for an old swing standard. In jazz, we call this a "line."

Try to figure out why the whole A section, except for the second measure, essentially uses a G major scale for improvisation.

Lady Swing

IMPROVISING VIOLIN

SUPPORT MATERIALS

Audio/Visual

I Got Rhythm Changes (Music Minus One: Volume 47): Jazz Aids

Swing, Swing Swing (Music Minus One: Volume 39): Jazz Aids

Texas and Swing Fiddle (cassette series taught by Matt Glaser): Homespun Tapes

Backup Trax, Swing and Jazz Volume I (cassette): Mel Bay Publications

Swing Fiddle (video taught by Paul Anastasio): Ridge Runner

Recommended Reading

Jazz Violin by Matt Glaser: Oak Publications

Western Swing Fiddle by Tracy Phillips: Oak Publications

Bob Wills Fiddle Book by Gene Merritts: Creative Concepts

Recommended Listening

Claude Williams, Summit '88: Huiksi Music

Early Jazz Violin (featuring South, Smith, Venuti, Grappelli, and others)

Part II, The Talking Violin: Improvised Music Collective

Reference Contact List

Jazz Aids 1-800-456-1388
c/o Jamey Aebersold, P.O. Box 1244C, New Albany, IN 47151

Homespun Tapes, 1-800-33-TAPES, P.O. Box 694, Woodstock, N.Y. 12498

Improvised Music Collective, P.O. Box 495, NY, NY 10024

Mel Bay Publications, Pacific, MI 63069

Oak Publications, 1-800-431-7187, c/o Music Sales, 5 Bellvale Rd., Chester, NY 10918

Creative Concepts, 410 Bryant Circle, Box 848, Ojai, CA 93024

Ridge Runner: 1-800-FRET PRO
Dept. FM-500, 84 York Creek Dr., Driftwood, TX 78619

Huiksi Music, P.O. Box 495, NY,NY 10024

JAZZ VIOLIN

At this point in your learning process, you have (I hope) incorporated some of the textural elements of the blues into your sound, made a transition from the stiff, symmetrical rhythms of classical playing into the fluid, hard-driving eighth notes of the swing style, and are beginning to have a sense of how to work with chord changes. (If not, it would be to your advantage to backtrack and work with the preceding units in the book.) Now it's time to move on into a more complex style of improvisation.

Jazz violin is an incredibly broad term with one strong commonality: the word "jazz" infers that the player has the ability to improvise over chord changes or a given modal or textural structure. There are many styles within jazz: swing, bebop, cool, modal, avant garde, and fusion, to name a few. The best way to develop expertise in any one of these types of music, is to listen listen listen to the great artists within that style! It's a language, and no amount of academic learning can replace hearing how the language is spoken by its practitioners.

In the beginning, as each style of jazz evolved, there were clear stylistic distinctions. Nowadays, young players have been exposed to all that's come before, and will tend to mix in together everything they've heard. Try to listen to as many recorded and live artists as possible to capture the essence of what makes their sound speak the way it does.

One Key A Day

If you're learning a new tune, you can make a list of the scales it requires for improvisation, and focus on one a day to develop greater facility on each. Use some of the warm-up exercises outlined in "Building a Foundation" to increase your facility. By the end of even a week, your improvisation will have improved dramatically because each scale will have become an intimate friend rather than a hazy territory on the fingerboard.

Also try to take a moment to mentally connect with all of the scales you're actually learning when you work on one key. For instance, if you're warming up in Gm, picture the key like a map on the fingerboard G to G as a minor scale, then picture those same notes F to F as an F major scale, C to C as a C7 scale, and so on. Use the following chart to gain an overview of the relationship between the scales derived from a major scale, and the scales derived from a melodic minor scale:

Scales and Chords Based on Major and Melodic Minor

Notice how the following scales and chords are derived from the C major (and then the C melodic minor) scale(s) simply by applying the key signature to each new scale. (The important chordal tones have been left solid.)

IMPROVISING VIOLIN

Developing Chromatic Motion

Even though jazz musicians spend an inordinate amount of time mastering the arpeggiated form of each chord, as well as the appropriate diatonic or pentatonic scale for each scale type, the use of chromatic passing tones helps create the jazz sound. Knowing when and where to use a chromatic passing tone is essential, however. For instance, if you are playing in the key of C7 (a C major scale with a flatted seventh) and you decide to raise the seventh as a chromatic passing tone, it will sound like you've just played a wrong note! If, on the other hand, you use a flatted

three to lead up to the major third, or a flatted five to lead to the perfect fifth, or if you transit from the A to the C by quickly moving through both chromatic tones in between, you should be quite pleased with the results. In summary, then, you must still know what the primary tones in the key are, and use chromatics—like a skateboard—as a mode of transportation.

It's best to start by practicing a regular chromatic scale in order to become accustomed to moving up and down the fingerboard in that manner. Keep finger pressure light and easy.

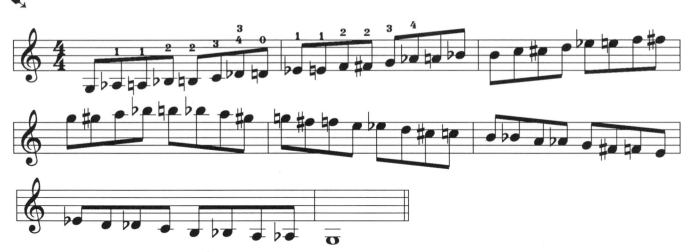

Now try a chromatic pattern, to help develop fluid motion chromatically. Make sure you keep your fingers in position, but release the active finger when it has double

duty (for instance: Eb to E) so that it floats along the surface of the string rather than dragging up or down.

Pick a key, and practice traveling up and down between primary tones.

Trampoline Fingers

Inflection (accentuation), phrasing (where you slur, and how you travel from note to note), and texture (how you color each note) is important in jazz. It can also be extremely subtle to explain and is sometimes best learned by listening to other players. One thing is certain, though: constant, even pressure will not yield a jazz sound on violin!

The following exercise will help you begin to vary finger pressure. Your bowing arm will respond to changes in left-hand finger pressure automatically because of how the brain tends to process information that is directed to one side and not the other (the brain's constant effort to include the opposite side of the body is sometimes, of course, undesirable when it comes to playing the violin):

Starting with your index finger on an "E" note on the D string, gently sink your finger down to the fingerboard and then slowly release it until the string is in its naturally relaxed position with the index finger touching its surface but not exerting any pressure. Practice going back and forth between these two extremes, and then move on to the next finger, and then the next, and so on. Since string width varies, it's valuable to repeat this process on each string.

Now choose a melodic line and try to vary each note of the melody by using a different amount of finger pressure, experimenting with the following possibilities:

1) start from a released position when you begin the note, or...

2) release while you're playing the note, or...

3) release when you're ready to move to the next pitch. Your first attempts to do this might sound too obvious or clumsy, but, when you least expect it, these new sounds will begin to become second nature to your technique.

Airplane Skids and Dips

In jazz, the bow rarely remains constant in its pressure or speed. To develop a wider palette of sounds, you must train your bowing arm to move in diverse ways.

Imagine that the string is a runway, and the bow is an airplane that keeps trying to take off; it rides along the runway, executes a smooth lift-off, and gently lands back down, all the while traveling at a consistent speed. I call this motion "airplane skids." When combined with trampoline fingers, the coarse, square edge of the notes are transformed into more of a cool, laid back "saxophone-esque" sound.

Now let the bow ride on the string with a normal, full volume. At regular intervals, dip the bow into the string while simultaneously moving the bow slightly closer to the bridge (to prevent a raspy tone). This "dip" in the sound can resemble a wave, and creates a nice subtle swell to the note when applied within a musical phrase.

Working with Chord Changes

Most jazz tunes are thirty-two bars in length. Each chord steers you into a different key and type of scale. For instance, if the tune opens with a Cm7 moving to an F7 in its first measure, then your improvisation will use a Cm7 scale for the first two beats, and an F7 scale for the following two beats. At first this seems overwhelming: not only do you have to learn the melody, but you also have to memorize the chord changes and switch keys and scale types at a split second pace. In addition to using the exercises in the "Building A Foundation" chapter, as well as the Introduction to this section, here are a some other techniques you can use to streamline this process.

Bridging Chord Changes

Beginners at improvisation will often start on the tonic of each chord change, but ultimately you want to create a through-thread between the harmonic changes. To work toward this goal, choose a tune and analyze the scales for similarities and differences. Try to spot which notes will flat or raise, and when. In the following example, I've used the first four measures of a jazz blues. Essentially, the scale moves from a Bb7 scale to a Bb minor scale and back again. Notice how the line I created over those changes doesn't stray far tonally when the chords change, but instead, draws upon the primary tones of each chord. ♪

Alternate Chord Exercise

Most tunes keep us moving through chord changes rapidly and we never get a chance to develop a more intimate knowledge of all the possible ways to transit from chord to chord. This exercise will help you to develop that facility.

Choose two consecutive chord changes from a tune you are currently working on. Set the metronome at a slow tempo, and start by playing four quarter notes (one note per tick) from the primary tones of

the first chord, and then the second chord. Keep oscillating back and forth between these two chords. Don't allow yourself to make large intervallic leaps. Try to really thread back and forth in a seamless fashion.

If you are doing well with this exercise using quarter notes, then try eighth notes, or only give yourself two beats per chord. Once you're threading fluidly, then repeat the exercise with the next two chords, and so on.

Most of the time, chords work together in chord cycles that are recognizable. There are a number of theory books that get into chord cycles and I've mentioned some of the best ones at the end of this chapter. We're going to look at one of the most common chord cycles, the II V I progression.

The V chord is almost always a dominant seventh chord (meaning that the seventh is flatted). Look through some tunes and spot the seventh chords. Most of the time you'll see that they lead to a I chord (which is usually major) or are preceded by a II chord (which is usually minor). While there are exceptions to this, the cycle is quite recognizable, and has been put together that way for a reason.

Imagine that you are playing on a tune that stays in C major for measures and measures. It gets boring. For greater harmonic interest, you add a Dm7 leading to a G7, and return to the CM. Now it's more interesting. Oddly enough, you've been in CM the whole time! The Dm7 and G7 chords have been altered in order to share common tones with CM, but their primary tones bring out new aspects of CM (D, F, A, C, and G, B, D, F) which help create a more interesting harmonic/melodic motion. If you didn't take the time to notice this inter-relationship, though, your mental process during improvisation would be choppier, more complicated, and lack continuity. Some musicians even choose to use only the one common scale for their improvisation over the cycle, making matters much simpler, but sometimes less sophisticated.

If you work on your II V I progression through all twelve keys, you will recognize these chord cycles every time they come up and be able to improvise with great expertise on the progression. Here's an exercise (you can use Jazz Aids, Volume 21, Disc #1, Cut #10 as an accompaniment) to help you get started:

Play the root note of each chord in the cycle. Keep moving down in fifths (or up in fourths) to start the new cycle for the new key:

Now try adding the third, fifth, and seventh of each chord. Apply this exercise to all twelve keys, moving through them chromatically, then through the cycle of fifths, and then in thirds, whole tone scales up and down, and so on (See "Building A Foundation"):

Exercise in I II V Key of C

At this point, it would be advantageous to take a few jazz standards and analyze them for the II V I progression. Then learn them using some of the exercises offered earlier in this chapter.

In "Building A Foundation," we examined the seven modes. Here's a tune that has been built on the A phrygian mode. As we discussed, the most difficult aspect of soloing on only seven notes, is to make the solo "tell a story."

Violinova
by Julie Lyonn Lieberman

6/8 feel over 2/4

♩ = 80

Solo using the A Phrygian Scale
in 2/4 using a triplet feel

Play tune in between solos and
then repeat once to end

1981 Huiksi Music

Atonal Versus Tonal

So far, we've only discussed tonal music. Tonal music is based on harmonic changes or a melodic tonal center. The solo on the following tune, Third Ear, however, is not based on either of these models. After the melody, it is entirely up to the soloist to weave an interesting solo based on whatever melodic, harmonic, textural, or rhythmic devices they so desire. This is extremely challenging because you must create a new structure each time you solo on this piece of music, and the structure must have its own integrity. Study the music of Billy Bang and Leroy Jenkins to hear some successful forays in this style.

Third Ear by Rez Abbasi

1993 Feroza Music

SUPPORT MATERIALS

Audio/Visual

There are dozens of recorded accompaniments available on cassette,
LP, or CD through Jazz Aids. Call for their catalogue.

Improvising Violin (a six-tape cassette series) by Julie Lyonn Lieberman: Homespun Tapes

Recommended Reading

Jazz Chord Studies by Matt Glaser: Berklee Press

Jazz Improvisation Made Easy (book and CD) by John Blake, Jr.: JIME

Techniques of Improvisation I, II, III, IV by David Baker: Alfred Publishing Company

Stringed Instruments Improvisation, Volumes I and II by David Baker: Alfred Publishing Co.

Jazz Violin by Matt Glaser: Oak Publications

Jazz Violin Studies by Usher Abell: Mel Bay Publications

Jazz Violin Styles by Dave Reiner and Glenn Asch: Mel Bay Publications

Recommended Listening

Early Jazz Violin, Violin of the Eighties, String Bands, New Age Strings :
The Talking Violin, Parts II, III, IV, and V: The Improvised Music Collective
Third Ear by Rez Abbasi, Ozone Records

Reference Contact List

Jazz Aids 1-800-456-1388
c/o Jamey Aebersold, P.O. Box 1244C, New Albany, IN 47151

Homespun Tapes, 1-800-33-TAPES, P.O. Box 694, Woodstock, N.Y. 12498

Improvised Music Collective, P.O. Box 495, NY, NY 10024

Mel Bay Publications, Pacific, MI 63069

Oak Publications, 1-800-431-7187, c/o Music Sales, 5 Bellvale Rd., Chester, NY 10918

JIME, P.O. Box 186, Littleton Rd., Westford, MA 01886

ROCK VIOLIN

Good rock string players have to develop a number of skills that differ from but are equally challenging to classical players. They should know how to improvise on chord changes; temper the width and speed of their vibrato to suit the desired effect; have a knowledge of fingerings and bowings that give most immediate access to the pentatonic and diminished pathways and lightning-fast bowings most often called for in rock music; be able to play on an amplified or electric instrument — sometimes one that has five strings; be well-versed in the right- and left-hand subtleties necessary to milk all of the possible textures and moods available; and be well versed in the use of electronic effects like chorus, flange, digital delay, and distortion. Rock players should also know how to use their instrument to create rhythmic backup so that they don't have to disappear in between solos.

There is a huge difference between the effect produced by background violins on rock tracks and the sound produced by a rock violinist. While the typically unimaginative use of the acoustic classical string section playing back-up to a rock song still dominates the industry, rock violinists like Mark Wood have clearly established rock violin as a sophisticated art form, destroying any preconceived notions we might have had that rock violinists are players who weren't good enough to succeed in classical music.

Playing In A Band

Many violinists are very excited to find themselves in their first band, only to discover that the other musicians in the band weren't trained in the academic sense of the word, and are finding their way through the music exclusively by ear. Therefore, questions like "What key are we in?" or "What are the chords to this tune?" might bring on looks of resentment or discomfort. Do the best you can by ear in this situation, and try to scope out a position close to the bass player or the keyboardist, or anyone who might be able to whisper some guidelines to you from time to time. Sometimes it's best to tape a few rehearsals and hash it out at home or with your private teacher. In either case, it's certainly a great forum for ear training!

On the other hand, you might find yourself in a band where the musicians are quite knowledgeable. They may place a chart in front of you that you don't understand. It's quite common to ask questions about the chart before playing it, but if you're in a situation where you don't feel comfortable doing that, then do the best you can by ear during the rehearsal and approach the leader or one of the other musicians afterwards. Playing in a band is like having a second family. You spend a lot of time together rehearsing, touring, and performing. Situations come up between personalities that need handling through communication. Generally, if you don't feel comfortable enough during the first few rehearsals to speak up, ask questions, and discuss the music, you might consider finding a different band to work with, where the musical environment is conducive to just such an exchange.

Developing Solid Solos

Just as we listen to our favorite classical string players to study their interpretation of the pieces we're working on, it's useful to study the solos of acclaimed or personally favorite rock artists. Don't limit yourself to violin solos. Include piano, sax, and guitar as well. Besides listening, it's quite helpful to learn to play some of their solos note for note to further develop your own playing abilities. Some musicians find it beneficial to learn to sing the solo first, before transferring it onto their instrument. To do this, it's easier to tape the solo a number of times consecutively on a cassette. Once you've learned the solo, you can try to jam with

the record. Approach it as if you were playing a duet with the soloist.

Role Models

Rock violinists such as Sugarcane Harris, Papa John Creach, Jerry Goodman, Randy Sabien, Jean Luc Ponty, Scarlet Rivera, L. Shankar, and Mark Wood are excellent role models to help develop a non-classical sound on the violin. It's also extremely helpful to listen to the early blues fiddlers and jazz violinists to get an idea of what's possible on the instrument.

I've discovered that even students who only want to learn classical repertoire have found many of the techniques and skills necessary for rock violin enjoyably freeing, and pertinent to their classical technique. Since I have devoted a whole separate chapter to amplification, this chapter will focus more on the stylistic and technical elements necessary for rock playing. Here are a few tips to help get you started:

ROCK TECHNIQUE

Some Technical and Musical Pointers

One of the biggest transitions from classical to rock is learning to create a wider range of textures and inflections. Rather than attacking each note cleanly and precisely, the genre calls for a much broader range of note-to-note transitions. Rock playing, in particular, requires either a slower and wider, or a faster, more hysterical vibrato.

Mark Wood suggests developing a fast spicatto (which he calls "hammered bowing")

and ricochet. These bowings, coupled with the use of distortion, are extremely effective in this style.

Fingerings tend to move horizontally (in position, across the four strings) just as much as vertically (moving up and down the fingerboard on one string), and often when players want to transpose a musical phrase, they will use their first finger as the root of the key or riff. This ability can be developed by creating a four or five-note musical phrase and moving it through the twelve keys, always starting with the first finger on the tonic (wherever the tonic appears in the riff).

It's also extremely helpful to learn to play bass lines. This can be done by copying them off of a recording to get a sense of how the bass player thinks and hears. This will help with transitions from purely melodic hearing and playing to rhythmic or harmonic hearing, which enables the player to accompany other soloists.

Right-Hand Rhythms

We are so conditioned by classical music to unconsciously view the bowing arm as a servant to the left-hand's lines, that it takes a bit of practice to develop an equal relationship between the two sides.

To begin this process, practice inventing rhythmic figures in your bowing arm, using only one note (or the open string). Mix rhythms, practice them at various tempos, and don't forget to use rests to help shape more interesting phrases. Once you've perfected a number of rhythmic phrases, try first playing the phrase on one note, and then repeating it by changing pitches on every bow change. (See *Building Foundation*)

Pentatonic Mastery Of The Keys

Pentatonic scales are five-note scales that are very popular in the blues and rock styles. They can also be useful in jazz. Five-note scales can be traced to India, China, and the Middle East, as well as other pockets of the world. It's most interesting to look at the Chinese approach to five-note scales. Since Chinese music is so integral to spirituality and political thought, and Chinese philosophy places great importance on balance (yin and yang), the notes in each of their five-note scales represent a complimentary unit. For instance, the notes of one scale might correspond to water, earth, air, sky and wind, while another might be associated with the North, South, East, West, and center.

I've included a number of patterns you can work on while learning the minor pentatonic scales in all twelve keys. (You can also apply all of these exercises to major pentatonic scales.) These exercises are useful within your improvisation, and help you to master the scales in as many different patterns as possible. While scales can be extremely helpful to establish the "layout of the land," patterns are an important stepping stone toward breaking out of diatonic (step-wise) movement into more fluid, melodic shapes. Therefore, familiarization with all possible fingered pathways on the fingerboard, (through scales and patterns) in all twelve keys, is a great preparatory step for improvisation in any style.

To develop a strong rhythmic ability, the following scales and patterns can also be practiced against a rock 'n roll back-beat supplied by a rhythm machine (Wood recommends using the Yamaha QY drum machine for this purpose). Note-to-note inflection or phrasing can be varied by experimenting with bow pressure and speed so that the note-to-note movement is not all the same volume and sound quality.

Pentatonic Scales

IMPROVISING VIOLIN

Pentatonic Pattern I

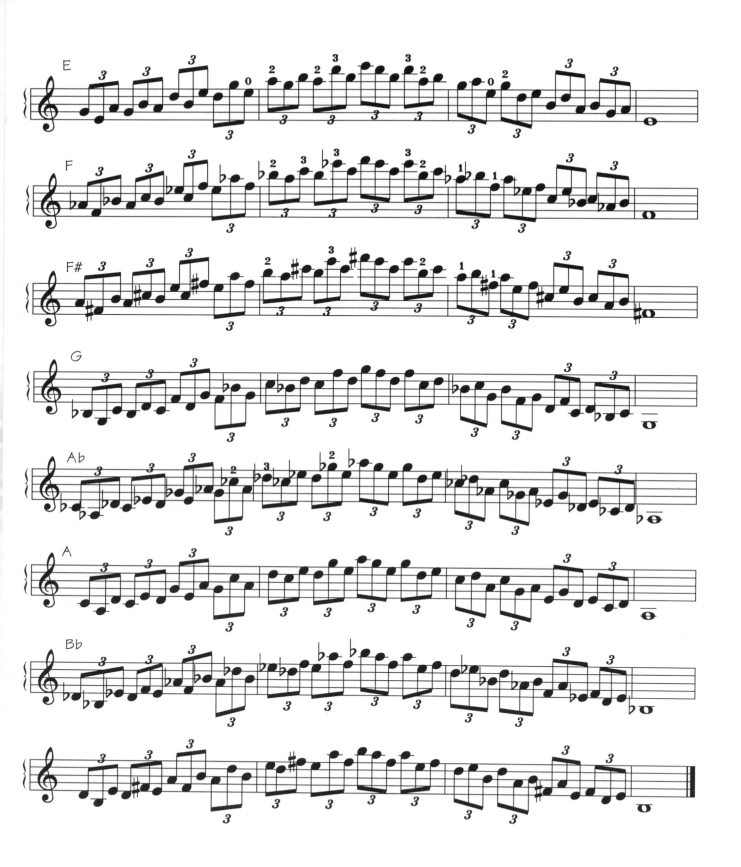

IMPROVISING VIOLIN

Pentatonic Pattern II

Transpose this pattern into all twelve keys.

Pentatonic Pattern III

Transpose this pattern into all twelve keys.

MARK WOOD

Diminished Arpeggios and Scales

Diminished arpeggios and scales are also popular in the rock idiom. The diminished arpeggio is comprised of all minor thirds, and the scale alternates whole with half steps.

Due to the tempered (measured and consistant) nature of the scale and arpeggio, once you learn one key, you've also learned three others. For instance, the key of C moves through the chord tones of C, Eb, F#, and A. Since the scale tones alternate whole and half steps, you could start on each of those pitches and construct a scale that would use the same notes as the other three chord tones.

Since there are so many flatted tones (b3, b5, bb7) to deal with, it's easier to con-

struct diminished chords and scales by thinking in intervals (whole/half/whole/half for the scale or minor thirds if you're playing the chord tones) rather than focusing on the key signature. In fact, you will have an easier time working through the twelve keys by using enharmonic names (pitch names that are not necessarily in the key: for instance, there is no F# in the key of C, and it's actually a b5 or Gb, but it might be easier for you to think of it in that context as an F#).

Once you've practiced the diminished chords and scales in all twelve keys by actually only playing three keys, then move on to practicing the patterns.

This exercise covers the keys of G, Bb, Db, and E. Once mastered,
it can be transposed into Ab (B, D, and F) and A (C, Eb, and F#).
Enharmonic names have been used to make note recognition easier
for you.

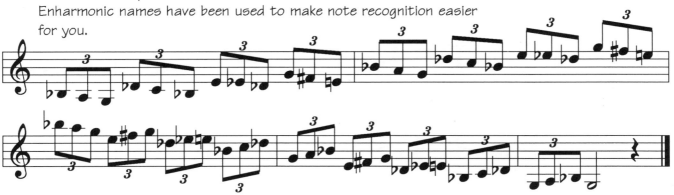

C diminished: Transpose this exercise into the keys of Db and D

C diminished: Tranpose this exercise into the keys of Db and D

The following exercise descends on a minor seventh chord and ascends on a diminished chord. Enharmonic names have been used to make note recognition easier for you.

Rock Riffs and Showmanship

Let's face it. If you want to sound impressive in this idiom, subtlety isn't always the best route. Rock often requires some "teeth," a good dose of showmanship, and a bag of tricks that make you look flashy. You have to know how to let it rip, and your persona on stage is just as important as your technical capability.

Make sure that you don't stand still like a wooden block while you are playing. I always tell my students to pretend that they are performing for an audience that is deaf, and that they somehow have to communicate the music through how they move on stage.

That exercise seems to bring great results every time!

There are also certain violinistic techniques that create an impressive effect: tremolo (a shimmer that's created at the tip of the bow, by moving it very quickly); fast double bows per note; patterns (such as the pentatonic patterns) run very quickly, usually culminating in a high note on the E string, with a wide, fast vibrato; and riffs (a three- or four-note figure that's repeated a number of times at a fast tempo) are all useful devices when it comes to sounding impressive!

Rock tunes often vary in structure, depending upon the composer and the style within the genre (gothic, heavy metal, pop, etc.). One element that's always consistant though, is that the structure revolves around best serving the lyrics. Since the lyrics are so central to the music, you must be careful when playing to never use busy lines over the lyrics; save them to use as fillers between lines or for your solo.

Blues

Since rock developed out of an earlier 12-bar, 3-chord musical form called the blues, it can be very useful to develop improvisational skills through learning the blues. This form also provides an opportunity to experiment with slides, pentatonic runs, and soloing on chord changes. (See Blues chapter.)

Improvisation

In non-classical music, the key signature only refers to the melody. Once one starts to improvise, the notes used for the solo are dictated by the chord symbols. (For example: A7 to DM means that you will use an A scale with a lowered seventh for the first measure, and then transition to the notes in D major for the next measure.) The warm-up should always include a review of these chord changes to master the keys involved in the particular song you are working on. This way, there will be greater freedom to move around the fingerboard in all possible appropriate note combinations without tremendous self-consciousness or awkwardness when improvising. Then you will be free to focus on hearing the line before playing it, and on trying to tell a story with the solo.

You will probably find that most of the chord changes, except during the chorus or any composed interludes, will boil down to the same seven notes, and that minor in rock or pop usually infers natural minor (b3, b6, and b7). For instance, if the chord changes say: CM, Dm, and Am, your scale tones will be derived from the C major scale, and you will not use an F# on the Am scale. Context is everything when it comes to figuring out exceptions. For instance, if you're in the key of GM and you come across an Am chord, you would use an F# in the scale, because GM uses it.

Back-up

Highly repetitious rhythmic figures, double stops, or long tones, are your best bet for backup. Since the violin's sound tends to cut through (once a solo instrument, always a solo instrument) you have to be really careful when you aren't soloing. For instance, only play fillers in between the vocalist's lines, and only if everyone else in the band isn't doing the same. Here are a few examples of typical backup lines:

To accompany the vocalist, repetitive rhythmic figures are the most unobtrusive:

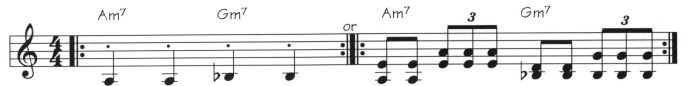

Here are some riffs you can practice. Try moving them through the popular rock keys: E, A, D, G, F, and C. See if you can guess what key each riff is in before you start transposition.

Solo in G minor

Audio/Visual

Dawg Tracks, Rock and Roll Back-up (cassette tape): Homespun Tapes

Blues in All Keys, Nothin' But Blues, Getting It Together, Major and Minor,
I Got Rhythm Changes (Music Minor One): Jazz Aids

Recommended Reading

Blues Fiddle by Julie Lyonn Lieberman: Oak Publications

Recommended Listening

The Talking Violin (Includes over 50 improvising violinists: Improvised Music Collective)

Voodoo Violince and *Against the Grain* featuring Mark Wood (see Discography)

Jean Luc Ponty, Randy Sabien, Sugarcane Harris, and Papa John Creach (see Discography)

Reference Contact List

Jazz Aids 1-800-456-1388
c/o Jamey Aebersold, P.O. Box 1244C, New Albany, IN 47151

Homespun Tapes, 1-800-33-TAPES, P.O. Box 694, Woodstock, N.Y. 12498

Improvised Music Collective, P.O. Box 495, NY, NY 10024

Oak Publications, 1-800-431-7187, c/o Music Sales, 5 Bellvale Rd., Chester, NY 10918

FOLK FIDDLE

Vassar Clements, Mark O'Connor, Darol Anger, and Matt Glaser are a few of the many violinists who started out as "fiddlers" and expanded into jazz styles. I always encourage my blues, jazz, and rock students to study various folk styles to help them learn how to swing rhythmically, and use syncopation, the shuffle stroke, cross-bow patterns, and fluid double stops. Folk styles can also help break the habit of using vibrato automatically, so that it can be used by choice as a seasoning.

While there are stylistic distinctions on violin between Irish, Cajun, old-timey, Western swing, bluegrass, and country music, we will not be looking into each style separately. Rather, this chapter is more concerned with the most important elements that make up a good folky sound on fiddle for improvisation within a folk band context.

Incidentally, there is no physical difference between a violin and a fiddle. We just use the term fiddle to imply that the style being played is folk. As for the difference between folk and country—that has more to do with the vocal style used, the instrumentation, and the outfits worn! As far as the use of the fiddle is concerned, there are stylistic distinctions, but there's more crossover than difference.

FOLK TECHNIQUE

The Shuffle Stroke

The shuffle stroke is a bow pattern that lies at the heart of the country or folk fiddle sound. The pattern consists of a long bow followed by two shorter bows. This usually takes place at the center or three-quarter section of the bow and is rarely written into a fiddle tune; you just have to be savvy enough to use it automatically when playing in a folk style. Make sure that you include the inflection (accent) on the weak part of the beat to make the bow stroke dance.

Fiddle Bowings

As we've discussed in the jazz and swing chapters, classical bowings tend to be more symmetrical while non-classical bowings will often accentuate the weak part of the beat, or emphasize diversification within each musical phrase. The following bowings can be applied to the folk style:

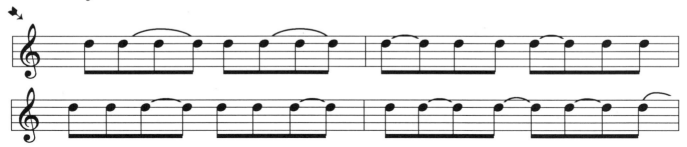

Cross Bow Patterns

In addition to the bowing patterns previously outlined, the old-timey fiddling style uses cross bow patterns that are quite effective when added into improvisations within the folk or country styles. Here are a few typical cross bow patterns. Practice them using your open strings first, and then add the left hand in. After you've played through these examples, use the bowing framework and come up with some of your own left-hand patterns.

Dips

There are many ways to travel with the bow when playing a note; you can send it spinning or ringing, you can give it a clean, light end, or you can wring it a little bit. In folk fiddling, that slight squeeze on the note is created by lightly dipping the bow into the string and making the note hover for a split second before moving on. While difficult to describe with words, you will recognize this sound if you listen to Mark O'Connor or Vassar Clements. There is a slightly drag on certain notes to accentuate them. This action should be created by leaning into the bow with the index finger, not by pressing the arm down.

In addition, you can create left-hand dips by leaning back a quarter tone and then returning to the original scale tone. Dip the bow into the string simultaneously. Try to lean your hand back a quarter tone rather than sliding it back.

Double Stops

Folk and country fiddling would be nothing without the use of double stops. This is when the fiddlers plays two notes at a time. The most commonly used double stops are those that combine the 1, 3, 5, or 6 of the key in various inversions. The best way to approach mastering double stops in all of the most popular folk keys—G, A, D, E, and F—is to work on one key at a time and start with your two lowest strings, searching out every possible combination; then move to the next two strings, and the next two. Unisons (the same note played against itself as in a fingered A against an open A) are extremely popular in this idiom, too, so don't leave them out.

As you work on your double stops, just remember that they are not created through excessive bow pressure, but rather through arm placement. The height of the arm should favor both strings simultaneously. If you get an "under-water" type sound, your bow is too close to the fingerboard, and if you get too much raspiness, move the bow a little faster, and lighten up.

Both Country and folk music are based on extremely simple chord progressions. Often one or two scales can be used throughout an entire tune, with the biggest harmonic change usually occurring during the bridge (or chorus). Here's an example of a typical tune. The notes written underneath each measure indicate what scale would become the basis of your improvisation. I've highlighted what I call the "pivot" notes. These are the pitches that are central to the harmonic progression taking place. The other scale tones are shared between the chords.

Surprise! The C is sharp to stay consistent with D major

The B minor is a natural minor scale (b3, b6, b7) to stay in the key of D major

SUPPORT MATERIAL

Audio/Visual

Cajun Fiddle (video) by Michael Doucet: Homespun Tapes

Contest Fiddling Championship Style (video) by Mark O'Connor: Homespun Tapes

The Fiddle According To Vassar (video) by Vassar Clements: Homespun Tapes

Recommended Reading

Vassar Clements by Matt Glaser: Oak Publications

Reference Contact List

Oak Publications, 1-800-431-7187, c/o Music Sales, 5 Bellvale Rd., Chester, NY 10918

Homespun Tapes, 1-800-33-TAPES, P.O. Box 694, Woodstock, NY 12498

NEW AGE VIOLIN

After the Beatles discovered the music of Ravi Shankar in the sixties and introduced the sounds of the sitar to the world on their Rubber Soul album, Indian music began to gain recognition in the United States. American listeners had increasing numbers of opportunities to appreciate the eastern sound through an influx of classical Indian records and performances, and through American artists like John McLaughlin, who began to integrate Indian sounds and concepts into their music.

As Indian gurus (spiritual teachers) became more prevalent in the United States, meditation began to be practiced by more and more Americans, and the marriage between aspects of Indian music, American instrumentation, and music as a relaxing, spiritually evocative force began to infiltrate the record industry (Windham Hill, among other labels) as well as the air waves (John Schaefer's "New Sounds").

NEW AGE VIOLIN TECHNIQUE

The question is, "What do violinists need to know in order to be able to play with artists like Kitaro or Andreas Wollenweider?" Perhaps our best approach to answering this question is to examine aspects of Indian music that might be useful to us.

The Indian approach to rhythm, form and improvisation is quite sophisticated and offers tremendous musical depth to those who study it. For instance, scales, ragas (melodic forms), and rhythms are learned vocally first, before the musician begins learning his or her instrument of choice. Since there are seventy-two scales in Indian music, 64,848 ragas, and 108 functional rhythms, the aural approach to learning ensures that the musician listens extremely carefully; a keen sense of pitch is developed through exercising relative pitch by singing/playing in relation to a drone (a held pitch).

In addition, in Indian music training, the technical, mental, and spiritual aspects of music-making receive equal emphasis.

Hindustani (Classical North Indian) and Karnatic (South Indian) approaches to music differ in that improvisation can be found only at the heart of Hindustani music, but training for both styles is extraordinarily rigorous.

Ravi Shankar, in his autobiography *My Music, My Life*, states that the Indian musician trains for twenty years; five of these years are spent living with the guru (music master), and during this time, the disciple studies seven days a week with few interruptions. His protege, Roóp Verma, told me that Indian musicians believe that they have a great responsibility: "They must be very careful with the sounds they create, because each micro-sound is responsible for creating a different mood, a psychological and physical condition."

The Western European violin has been used in India for many centuries. The Indian violin, the *saragi*, has one brass string, three gut strings, and twenty-three strings that are not bowed, called sympathetic strings because they vibrate in sympathy with the bowed tones. The European violin, which arrived with Western explorers over two hundred years ago, is usually tuned C G C G, or A D A D. It's held differently than in the West; the player sits cross-legged and the scroll is placed against the ankle. The back of the violin is rested on the left shoulder and collarbone or chest. This leaves the left hand free to play embellishments.

Let's take a look at some of the ingredients of Indian music that make up the artist's vocabulary for improvisation.

Ornamentation and Embellishment

There are a total of fifteen kinds of grace notes (gamakas) in Indian music, as well as many other methods of adding texture to the notes of a raga. Ravi Shankar says that "…in our music, the transition from one tone to another is never made directly, as in most of Western music; a subtle ornament, a kind of gliding, is added to soften and mellow the movement. The ornaments are not arbitrarily attached to a melody; rather, they seem to grow out of it…Indian music is characterized by gentle curves, controlled grace, minute twining, winding whorls of detail."

Ornaments require enormous agility in the left hand as well as excellent right- to left-

hand coordination. You will find that in order to even approach the gliding described by Ravi Shankar, you will have to teach your left hand particularly the thumb and arm to be extremely relaxed while playing.

Vicki Horner Richard's, in her article for "Journal of the Violin Society of America" titled *An Interview with Dr. N. Rajam*, wrote that her teacher, Dr. N. Rajam, says she uses "…special movements of the fingers to execute the 'graces' and ornamentations characteristic of Indian music. This involves sliding movements of the fingers on the fingerboard. In my technique I constantly glide in various patterns. There are many types of glide movements, and each type has its own considerable number of variations. The proper understanding of these variations, and the correct choice of them to suit the melody and mood desired, constitute the real goal of the training. It may take from six to eight years for a diligent student to achieve a good grasp of this style."(Vicki Horner Richards, The Violin in India, Journal of the Violin Society of America, Summer 1979, p. 138)

L. Shankar provides some further insights into Indian violin technique: "The Indian system of shifting and use of positions up the fingerboard is very different from the Western system. We don't always use principles like the guiding finger. Indian music has more pure notes; we rarely use vibrato. I think, from an intonation standpoint, that western violinists would benefit from practicing shifting without vibrato. It's too easy to use vibrato as a crutch; if you get to a note and it's out of tune, you just shake more!...In India, we often practice with a drone in the background, so you're practicing against something. This strengthens the relative intonation. (Matt Glaser, "An Interview with L. Shankar," The Oak Music Report, Spring 1981, p. 21)

For years, the violin in India had been used almost exclusively to provide melodic accompaniment in vocal concerts. Vicki Richards points out that "...the influence of the vocal style on violin playing in India has resulted in the evolution of a left-hand technique totally different from that of the Western classical tradition. Movements from note to note, which sound like continuous glissandi, reveal a close connection to vocal tonal qualities and capabilities for expression." Only recently, through the evolution of a more advanced technique, has the violin emerged as one of the most important solo instruments in Indian music.

Innovative players such as the brothers L. Shankar and L. Subramaniam have brought their expertise from years of study of Indian violin over to the States. They have contributed to the development of violin technique through innovative bowing and left-hand work. They have also learned Western music and explored new ways of joining Indian and Western music.

It is best to listen to Indian music to hear and feel the ornamentation first hand. Here are a few exercises Subramaniam uses to help Western violinists master the technical aspects of ornamentation (as notated by Matt Glaser). Using either the upper or lower neighboring pitch from the scale...

Choose a scale and apply the following two rhythmic phrases to each note of the scale:

Rhythm

Indian time theory, codified after hundreds of years of experimentation, is extraordinarily sophisticated. Altogether, there are 108 functional (in everyday use) rhythms, with 15 to 20 in constant use. The measure, which can often be as long as sixteen beats, is subdivided into varying combinations. The even numbers are called fundamental; the odd, abstract. A measure containing eight beats can be subdivided as follows (In Indian notation, the beats are grouped by number with a dot in between; this indicates that an accent must be placed on the first beat of each grouping):

2·3·3 or **5·3** or **4·4**

In New Age music, however, the meters used tend to be in standard Western European meter, with, perhaps, some pieces in 5/4, 3/4, or 7/8. Therefore, it is to your advantage, if you wish to develop greater rhythmic expertise, to purchase a rhythm machine and program it to provide you with some more challenging meters so that you can practice soloing in them.

NEW AGE VIOLIN STRUCTURE

While in India, the musicians choose their scales and ragas (melodic structures) very carefully—each group of notes are believed to correspond with a particular time of day, mood, or emotion. You are less likely to come across this in commercial New Age music! Each composer has their own approach to structure (length, sections, etc.), and a lot of the music is either soothing or meditational in nature, or highly rhythmic and celebratory, but either stylistic foundation will tend to be structured around one or two tonal centers.

Here are two solos for you to study. The first one exemplifies how you might approach a meditational piece based on the D Lydian mode. The second explores that same mode over a fast, driving rhythmic pulse.

©1993 Huiksi Music

Solo in D

♩ = 120 Play against a rhythmic background with a D pedal point:

SUPPORT MATERIALS

Recommended Listening

New Age Violin, Part IV of The Talking Violin: The Improvised Music Collective

L. Shankar, L. Subramaniam, Vicki Richards (see Discography)

Reference Contact List

The Improvised Music Collective, P.O. Box 495, NY, NY 10024

EPILOGUE

I thought it fitting to close this book with an excerpt from Dave Balakrishnan's recorded work, Spider Dreams (Windham Hill, WH 01934 10141-2). Originally written for symphony orchestra, this score is a string quartet reduction excerpted from the seven-movement work.

Balakrishnan embodies everything we've covered in this book. His music comes from his heart and soul, yet is grounded in a deep and lengthy study of theory, composition and technique. He has embraced all styles of music compositionally as well as in performance on violin. I heartily recommend that you listen to this work in its entirety.

If you are interested in exploring more arrangements and originals for jazz string ensemble, including much of the repertoire of the Turtle Island String Quartet, you can write for a free catalogue: Spleehab Music, P.O. Box 23963, Pleasant Hill, CA 94523.

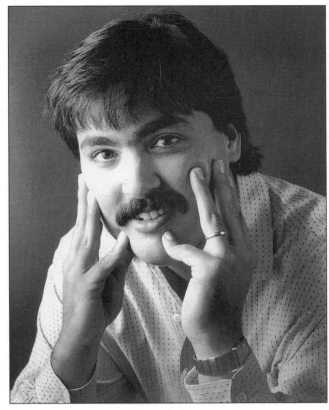

DAVE BALAKRISHNAN

SPIDER DREAMS

by Dave Balakrishnan

© 1992 Spleehab Music, all rights reserved.

Used by permission.

Spiderdreams by Dave Balakrishnan

IMPROVISING VIOLIN

IMPROVISING VIOLIN

IMPROVISING VIOLIN

DISCOGRAPHY

Please note: This discography does not profess to contain every jazz violin record ever made; some recordings listed here may even be out of print. For an excellent overview of over fifty improvising violinists, see the order form on page 130 for The Talking Violin. For a complete discography on every blues fiddler ever recorded, consult my book, "Blues Fiddle."

Ali, Akbar
Black Swan Quartet, Minor Music LC 8847
Anger, Darol (see Turtle Island String Quartet)
The Duo, Rounder Records 0168
Tideline, Windham HIll 1021
Chiaroscuro, Windham HIll 1043
Fiddlistics, Kaleidoscope Records F-8
Psychograss, Windham Hill 01934 11132-2
Asmussen, Svend
Hot Fiddle, Brunswick 58051
Hot Swing Fiddle Classics, Folklyric Records 9025
Toots and Svend/Yesterday and Today, A&M SP 3613
Svend Asmussen: Amazing Strings, MPS 20 22373 6
Svend Asmussen Spielt Welterfolge, Telefunken NT 421
Duke Ellington's Jazz Violin Session, Atlantic SD 1688
Skol, Epic 3210
Prize Winners, Matrix 1001
Bacsik, Elek
Bird and Dizzy, Flying Dutchman BDL 1-1082
I Love You, Bob Thiele Music BBL1-0556
Bang, Billy
New York Collage, Anima 40620
Sweet Space, Anima 12741
Distinction Without A Difference, Hat Hut 04
Rainbow Gladiator, Soul Note 1016
Invitation, Soul Note 1036
Outline No. 12, Celluloid 5004
Bangception, Hat Music 3512
Fire From Within, Soul Note 1086
Live at Carlos, Soul Note 121136
Valve No. 10, Soul Note 121186
Tribute to Stuff Smith, Sept. 1992
Blake, Jr., John
Maiden Dance, Gramavision 8309
Rhythm and Blues, Gramavision 8608
New Beginning, A, Rhino 79455
Adventures of the Heart, Gramavision 18-8705-1
Bluestone, Harry
Artistry in Jazz, Dobre DR 1011
Brown, Clarence Gatemouth
Clarence Gatemouth Brown, Blackjack 9002
Clarence Gatemouth Brown: The Original Peacock Recordings, Rounder Records 2039
Clements, Vassar
Vassar Clements, Mercury SRM-1-1022
Compo, Peter
Notalgia in Time Square, Cadence Jazz CJR 1038
Live at the West End Cafe, Bean Records 101
Creach, Papa John
Papa John Creach, Grunt FTR-1003
Rock Father, Buddah 0698
Playing My Fiddle For You, Grunt BLF 1-0418

Goodman, Jerry
Ariel, Private Music 2013
Glaser, Matt
Jazz Violin Celebration (with Darol Anger and Dave Balakrishnan), Kaleidoscope F-22
Play Fiddle Play, Flying Fish 70555
Grappelli, Stephane
Django Reinhardt & Stephane Grappelli (Hot Club of France) RCA 731.042, serie Black & White Vol. 32, Victor
Parisian Swing, Vintage Series GNP 9002
Django Reinhardt, Vogue, CLD 813
Tea for Two, Angel 37533
Violins No End (with Stuff Smith), Pablo 2310-907
Feelings and Finesse = Jazz, Atlantic 1391
I Remember Django, Black Lion 105
Limehouse Blues, Black Lion 760158
Grappelli Meets Barney Kessel, Black Lion 760150
Venupelli Blues, Charly 73
Homage to Django, Classic Jazz 23
Just One of Those Things, Angel 69172
Parisian Thoroughfare, Black Lion 760132
Stuff and Slam, Accord 233076
Reunion with George Shearing, Polygram 21868
Stephane Grappelli/Bill Coleman, Classic Jazz 24
Live at Carnegie Hall, Doctor Jazz 38727
Young Django, Veve i15672
Live at Tivoli Gardens, Pablo 441
Stephane Grappelli and Hank Jones, Muse 5287
Stephane Grappelli and David Grisman Live, Warner Brothers 3550
Happy Reunion, Rhino 79242
At the Winery, Concord Jazz 4139
Live at San Francisco, Black Hawk 51601
Together at Last, Flying Fish 421
Grappelli Plays Jerome Kern, GRP 9542
One on One with McCoy Tyner, Milestone 9181
In Tokyo, Denon 9130
Stephane Grappelli Meets Earl Hines, Black Lion 760168
Paris Encounter, Atlantic
Shades of Django, Verve 825955
Grappelli, Louis Bellson and Phil Woods, Rushmore 3000
Fascinating Rhythm, ONyx Classix 267329
Menuhin and Grappelli Play "Jalousie," Angel 69220
Afternoon in Paris, BASF, MPS 20876
Stephane Grappelli 1971, PYE Popular NSPL 18360
Stephane Grappelli 1973, PYE Popular NSPL 18403
Harris, Sugarcane
Cup Full of Dreams, MPS MB-21792
Hwang, Jason
Caverns, New World 80458-2
Jenkins, Leroy
For Players Only, JCOA 1010

Solo Concert, India Navigation
Lifelong Ambitions, Black Saint 0033
Legend of Ai Glatson, Black Saint 22
Space Mind/New Worlds, Tomato 8001
Mixed Quintet Black Saint 0060

Kennedy, Jr., Joe
Where've You Been?, Concourd Jazz 145
Magnifique!, Black & Blue WE 341
Trends, Asch Recordings Disc 707

Kindler, Steve
Private Music Label

LaFlamme, David
Inside Out, Amherst Records AMH 1012

Levine, Michael
No Guitars, CMI Music

Lockwood, Didier
The Didier Lockwood Group, Gramavision 18-8412-1

O'Connor, Mark
Heroes, Warner Bros. 9 45257-2

Pointer, Noel
Hold-on, United Artists UA-LA848-H 0798
Phantazia, Blue Note

Ponty, Jean Luc
Violin Summit (with Smith, Grappelli, Asmussen), Verve 821303
Cantelope Island, Blue Note 632
New Violin Summit, MPS8
Upon the Wings of Music, Atlantic 18138
Jean Luc Ponty and Stephane Grappelli, Verve 835320
Sunday Walk, BASF 20645
Enigmatic Ocean, Atlantic SD 19110
Electric Connection, World Pacific Jazz 20156
The Jean-Luc Ponty Experience, World Pacific Jazz ST-20168
Aurora, Atlantic SD 18163
Upon the Wings of Music, Atlantic SD 18138
Cosmic Messenger, Atlantic SD 19189
Imaginary Voyage, Atlantic SD 18195

Richards, Vicki
Parting the Waters, Third Stream Music CD 1001
Quiet Touch, New Age Records 425
Live in India, New Age Records 812

Sabien, Randy
Fiddlehead Blues, Fiddlehead Music
The Sound of Fish Dreaming, Fiddlehead Music

Seifert, Zbigniew
Passion, ST 11923

Shankar, L.
Shakti (John McLaughlin), "A Handful of Beauty," Columbia 34372
Who's To Know, ECM

Smith, Stuff
Swinging Stuff, Storyville 4087
Stuff Smith and His Onyx Club Boys, Classics 706
Stephane Grappelli and Stuff Smith, Verve 8270
Live in Paris, FCD 120
Live at Montmartre, Storyville 4142
Stuff Smith, Everest Records FS-238
The 1943 Trio, Circle CLP-132
Black Violin, MPS 20650
Hot Swing Fiddle Classics, Folklyric 9025
Have Violin Will Swing, Verve MGV 8282
Stuff Smith, Verve MGV 8206
Dizzy Gillespie/Stuff Smith, Verve MGV 8214

Soldier String Quartet
Sequence Girls, Rift 13

South, Eddie
The Chronological Eddie South 1937 -1941, Classics 737
Eddie South: Black Gipsy, Jazz Archives No. 70, 157942
Djangologie #5 and #6, EMI Pathe CO54 16004 and CO 54 16006

String Trio of New York
Area Code 212, Black Saint 0048
As Tears Go By, ITM 0048
Ascendant, Vintage Jazz 532
Octagon, Black Saint 120131-2

Subramaniam, L
Spanish Wave, MIlestone 9114
Indian Express, MIlestone 9120
Blossom, Crusaders CRP-16003
Magic Fingers, Ganesh Records DRLS 4003
Indian Classical Music, Discovery Records, DS-202
Inde Du Sud, Musidisc 558585/86
Subramaniam, MAI: 8107

Sugarcane Harris
USA Union (John Mayall), Polydor 0704

Taylor, Will
RadioEdge, Will Taylor Productions

Turtle Island String Quartet
Spider Dreams, Windham Hill 10141-2
Turtle Island String Quartet, Windham Hill 0110
Metropolis, Windham Hill 0114
Skylife, Windham Hill WD 0126
On the Town, Windham Hill Jazz 10132-2
Who Do We Think We Are? Windham Hill Jazz 10146-2

Uptown String Quartet
Uptown String Quartet, Philips 838 358-2

Urbaniak, Michal
Fusion, Columbia 32852
Cinemode, Rykodisc 10037
Music for Violin and Jazz Quartet, JAM 001

Venuti, Joe
Joe Venuti with Eddie Lang, JSP 10
Joe Venuti and His Violin, Jazz Man 336
Violin Jazz, Yazoo 1062
Stringing the Blues, Sony Special Products 24
Mad Fiddler from Philly, Shoestring
Venupelli Blues, BYG 529122
Daddy of the Violin, MPS 5050
Joe & Zoot, Chiaroscuro 128
Blue Four, Chiaroscuro 134
Hot Sonatas, Chiaroscuro 145
Sliding By, Gazell 1014
Joe in Chicago, Flying Fish 077

White, Michael
Father Music, Mother Dance, Impulse AS-9268
Impulse Artists on Tour, AS-9264
Spirit Dance, Impulse AS-9215

Williams, Claude
Live at J's Part 1 & 2, Arhoolie 405, 406
Summit '88, Huiksi Music 02
The Man From Muskogee, Sackville 3005

Wood, Mark
Voodoo Violince, Guitar Recordings 88561-5040-2
Against the Grain, Guitar Recordings, 9714-99403-2

INDEX

Books and Videos
by Julie Lyonn Lieberman

You Are Your Instrument: The Definitive Musician's Guide To Practice and Performance

Only a handful of musicians know how to create music in a fluid, pain-free manner. *You Are Your Instrument* is a comprehensive, fully illustrated, 152-page reference book designed to teach musicians how to develop a more effective as well as enjoyable experience during practice and performance, and how to heal existing injuries.

Here's what over 35 reviewers have to say about this international best-seller: "...an exceptional title...well-written...comprehensive...a must-have...an invaluable vehicle for musicians who want to learn to use their bodies and minds more intelligently while practicing and performing...her six-level approach to memorization is worth the price of the book...it should be on the shelf of every musician who wants to play without pain." ($20.00)

Improvising Violin

Put fire in your bow! Written for the violinist who longs to leave the confines of the written page, *Improvising Violin* is a comprehensive guide to the art of violin improvisation in jazz, blues, swing, folk, rock, and New Age. This 132-page book offers dozens of exercises, riffs, stylistic techniques, patterns, chord charts, tunes, photos, quotes and anecdotes, with a preface by Darol Anger. ($19.95)

Planet Musician

With more than 150 world scales and modes, mental and technical exercises, *Planet Musician* offers a fresh approach to music making. This innovative publication offers exciting ways for players to enrich their own musical styles by integrating ideas, techniques, and sounds from musical traditions from around the world. Comes with a 74-minute practice CD. ($23.95)

Rockin' Out With Blues Fiddle

The blues provides a support structure and environment for incredibly powerful improvisation, especially for violinists. After all, the violin is capable of bending, sliding, moaning, whispering, and more; the violin is the closest to the voice of any instrument. This book, with its supportive practice CD, can take you from anonymous interpretive artist to expressive soloist by helping you unlock your musical imagination, fine-tune your right- and left-hand touch, and, most importantly, create your own, unique blues sound. ($21.95)

The Contemporary Violinist

With the support of a practice CD, you will be guided through exercises and tunes designed to help you develop a feel for playing sixteen styles, including Latin, Flamenco, Gypsy, Tango, Klezmer, Cajun, Blues, Rock, Swing, Bebop, Country, Irish, Old-Time, Bluegrass, Franco-American, and Scandinavian.

This book offers seventeen tunes; dozens of left- and right-hand exercises and techniques; extensive information on each style as well as how to improvise in each genre; instrument care; new approaches to maximizing practice time; fiddle camps; equipment tips; playing healthy; fiddle on the internet; and fiddle horror stories!

With inspiring advice from Jean-Luc Ponty, Buddy Spicher, Mary Ann Harbar, Matt Glaser, James Kelly, Martin Hayes, Bruce Molsky, Jay Ungar, Mark Wood, Betsy Hill, Joe Kennedy, Jr., John Hartford, Randy Sabien, Claude Williams, Richard Greene, Stacy Phillips, Darol Anger, Michael Doucet, Leif Alpsjö, Yale Strom, Alicia Svigals, Willie Royal, Donna Hébert, Natalie MacMaster, Papa John Creach, Anthony Barnett, and Sam Zygmuntowicz! ($23.95)

The Instrumentalist's Guide to Fitness, Health, and Musicianship

With special guests Barry Mitterhoff (mandolin/guitar), John Blake, Jr. (violin), David Krakauer (clarinet), and Sumi Tonooka (piano), as well as physical fitness trainer Michael Schwartz, Julie Lyonn Lieberman offers an ergonomic approach to music making that boosts whole-brain thinking and improves playing. You'll learn breathing and stretching techniques, warm-ups and cool-downs, and self-massage, as well as exercises to relax and center you. You'll see and feel how tension negatively affects your playing and learn how to eliminate it. 90-minute video. ($39.95)

The Vocalist's Guide to Fitness, Health, and Musicianship

Julie Lyonn Lieberman and three highly respected experts – Maitland Peters, Katie Agresta, and Jeannie Deva – share valuable tips and hands-on tools to successfully counteract common problems faced by vocalists. In a simple, direct way, each offers advice and practice techniques addressing such important issues as breath support and control, vocal stamina, the causes of vocal dysfunction and injury, effective warm-ups and cool-downs, and the effect of diet and the environment on the body's ability to produce sound well. A lesson in vocal anatomy is included. 90-minute video. ($39.95)

The Violin in Motion: An Ergonomic Approach to Playing for all Levels and Styles

Take a 60-minute private lesson with Julie Lyonn Lieberman on video. Her unique approach challenges the age-old "do as I do," offering violinists and violists a physiological basis for building effortless, fluid technique based on individual body type.

Sections include: holding the bow and the violin based on ergonomics; bridging from a static relationship into one that constantly breathes; the motor cortex and its relationship to music-making; factoring in your body-type when building technique; dozens of key technical tips; and a ten-minute exercise program designed specifically for violinists and violists! 60-minute video. ($39.95)

Techniques for the Contemporary String Player

The string community is in the midst of a stylistic metamorphosis. Scores are incorporating scales, rhythms, ornaments, and textural ideas from the music of the world. Over 18 string styles have surged in popularity, including blues, swing, rock, old time, Celtic, Cajun, Cape Breton, Flamenco, Gypsy, and Latin.

Whether you want to learn a new style, be ready for anything that comes up at a jam session, or meet the demands of new orchestral scores with ease, Julie Lyonn Lieberman will help you develop the necessary skills. She has examined the technical demands of all the alternative styles and organized the most essential right- and left-hand skills into these videos.

Designed for violinists, violists, and cellists. ($34.95 each, $60 for the set)

Part One: The Bow Hand

Four essential bow control techniques, ten approaches to rhythmizing the bow, contemporary techniques to make each note speak, and much more!

Part Two: The Left Hand

Ten approaches to ornamentation, stylizing vibrato, use of double-stops, working with chords, slide techniques, a contemporary approach to navigating the fingerboard, and lots more!

Alternative Strings: The New Curriculum

By Julie Lyonn Lieberman

208 pp, over 50 illustrations, includes a CD, photos, and musical examples, 6" x 9" ©2004, softcover, ISBN # 1-57467-089-1, $24.95 plus shipping and handling

Available from Hal Leonard Corporation: 800-554-0626
Also available at www.amadeuspress.com

"Why can't the learning experience—from the middle school classroom to the conservatory—offer a process of exploration, discovery, creativity, and joyfulness while making music?" challenges celebrated improvising violinist Julie Lyonn Lieberman in the introduction to Alternative Strings: The New Curriculum. For practicing musicians, amateur and professional, classical string teachers and conductors, Lyonn Lieberman's seventh book is a must-have definitive resource guide designed to "stretch" traditional classical studies, and, as she notes, to "embrace the musical imagination of the world." It is crafted specifically to help promote diversity in strings through the inclusion of vernacular and world styles.

Readers will learn more about the origins of "alternative strings," a "catch phrase" for nearly 30 folk, world, jazz, and popular styles within a historical, stylistic and technical overview. Lyonn Lieberman enhances the book with detailed descriptions of over two dozen styles, abundant support materials, and a massive discography. Drawing upon more than three decades of experience as an alternative strings teacher and a performer, she also brings her early classical violin studies and what she describes in the introduction to her book as her "constant exposure" to blues, world music and American vernacular, to string educators and the 21st century string pedagogy.

Alternative Strings: The New Curriculum also addresses issues such as tradition versus innovation, the National Standards in relationship to improvisation and the inclusion of non-classical styles in the classroom, how to cultivate a rhythmic bow-hand, as well as the complex emotional/psychological issues associated with exploring new directions in a previously heavily codified field.

As an added bonus, the book is accompanied by a music and interview CD featuring fourteen of today's top alternative string players and clinicians including Mark Wood, Richard Greene, and Bob Phillips. These featured players demonstrate rock, jazz and fiddle styles, and present innovative ideas for teaching new generations of string players.

Clinics and Residencies with Julie Lyonn Lieberman

Julie Lyonn Lieberman brings over 25 years of expertise as an educator and performer to her private and group teaching. A dynamic, participatory workshop leader, her ability to stimulate participants to think and grow in new ways has earned respect for her work throughout the world.

Ms. Lieberman has presented for organizations, such as:
MENC: the National Association for Music Education; IAJE: the International Association of Jazz Educators; TODA: Texas Orchestra Director's Association; Suzuki Association; NOW: National Organization for Women; ASTA: American String Teacher's Association; and National Young Audiences.

Her clinics and residencies have taken place in such institutions as: Juilliard College of Music; Eastman Conservatory; Manhattan School of Music; the National String Workshop; the International String Workshop; The Mark O'Connor Fiddle Camp; New York University; New York Open Center; University of Stanford Jazz Workshop; The New School Jazz Program; Berklee College of Music; The Royal Academy of Music in Toronto, Canada; Centre for Human Performance & Health; Madeline Island Chamber Music Camp, Unison Learning Center; Cedar Rapids Symphony Orchestra; William Paterson College Jazz Department; New England Conservatory; University of Montevallo; Con Edison (upper management); and McGill University, as well as high schools and middle schools throughout the country.

Styles Survey (1 to 2 hours)
An overview of the alternative string field, including handouts listing all styles, how to access references, and a listening survey of the major styles as follows: Listening examples presenting master artists on CD for each major string style followed by a brief definition of the attributes and right- and left-hand figures that comprise that style, taught through demonstration and call and response.

Rhythmizing the Bow (60 – 90 minutes)
Chop technique, ostinatos, bass lines, two against three, syncopation, inflections, whip-bow, shuffle stroke, string-crossing patterns, and more!

Playing Healthy (1 to 2 hours)
An in-depth survey of muscle and joint function in relationship to practice and performance. Warning signs, healing approaches, fluid brain-to-muscle techniques, seated and standing posture, muscle balance exercises, and breathing techniques are covered. Plenty of time is allotted for questions and individual coaching (if time allows).

The Creative Band and Orchestra (1 to 2 hours)
This session presents dozens of techniques designed to stimulate creativity and improvisation without concern for harmonic or stylistic structures. These techniques can be used with students of all ages and levels with tremendous success.

Stylistic Improvisation (1 to 2 hours)
Three approaches to improvisation are covered during this session: melodic, modal, and harmonic. The harmonic segment can be tailored to the styles of your choice (blues, rock, folk, swing, and/or jazz)

Planet Musician (1 to 2 hours)
Odd meter, alternating meter, world scales, world practice techniques, distinctions and similarities between cultures, with listening examples and hands-on exercises.

Open Reading Session (60 to 90 minutes)
Ms. Lieberman presents orchestra charts in a number of alternative string styles to give teachers a chance to hear samples of material available and choose the most appropriate pieces for their level orchestra.

Soundstory and Performance Residencies
with Julie Lyonn Lieberman

Julie Lyonn Lieberman can be booked in a one-day, three-day or five-day package to help your group develop the performance of an original soundstory created by either your ensemble or by her.

A pre-supplied package: The Hobo Violin or The Roaring Brook Fiddler

A Lieberman soundstory consists of charts, a written story, and a brief, step-by-step training manual to help you get started. If Ms. Lieberman has to modify a pre-existing package to your needs, she requires a three-month lead-time to supply the charts. After you've had a chance to teach the charts to your students, she helps them during her residency to develop the improvised elements during the days leading up to the performance. The score and story can be modified appropriate to the playing level and ethnic backgrounds of your students or players. The residency culminates in a live performance that can include her as a narrator and/or soloist.

An Original Soundstory

Ms. Lieberman can also come to your institution to help your players develop their own, original soundstory by teaching them how to develop compositions and a storyline, as well as helping them develop their improvisatory skills. The residency culminates in a live performance that can include her as a narrator and/or soloist.

Performance Residency

Ms. Lieberman can present a 90-minute program, titled *The Talking Violin*, which covers styles from around the world and illustrates the five approaches to improvisation covered in this book. She can precede or follow this presentation with a training workshop for your ensemble in genre-specific improvisation.

**If you are interested in sponsoring a clinic or residency,
you can contact Ms. Lieberman via Email at:
Julie@JulieLyonn.com or by calling 212-724-3256**

**Julie Lyonn Lieberman
c/o Huiksi Music
P.O. Box 495
New York, NY 10024**